ECONOMIC HISTORY

THE INDUSTRIES OF LONDON SINCE 1861

BUSINESS HISTORY

THE INDUSTRIES OF LONDON
SINCE 1861

P.G. HALL

Routledge
Taylor & Francis Group

LONDON AND NEW YORK

First published in 1962

Published in 2006 by
Routledge
2 Park Square, Milton Park, Abingdon, Oxfordshire OX14 4RN
711 Third Avenue, New York, NY 10017

First issued in paperback 2014

Routledge is an imprint of the Taylor and Francis Group, an informa business

British Library Cataloguing in Publication Data
A CIP catalogue record for this book
is available from the British Library

The Industries of London Since 1861
ISBN 0-415-38158-4 (volume)
ISBN 0-415-37796-X (subset)
ISBN 0-415-28619-0 (set)

ISBN13: 978-1-138-86511-2 (pbk)
ISBN13: 978-0-415-38158-1 (hbk)

Routledge Library Editions: Economic History

MILES
0   8

COUNTY
BOUNDARIES

FULHAM = Metropolitan Boroughs

EALING = Municipal Boroughs,
Urban & Rural Districts

CHESHUNT

ELSTREE   POTTERS BAR

WALTHAM HOLY CROSS

ENFIELD

BUSHEY

BARNET

EAST BARNET

SOUTHGATE

EDMONTON

CHINGFORD

CHIGWELL

HENDON

FINCHLEY

WOOD GREEN

TOTTENHAM

WALTHAMSTOW

WANSTEAD & WOODFORD

ILFORD

RUISLIP NORTHWOOD

HARROW

HORNSEY

LEYTON

DAGENHAM

WEMBLEY

HAMPSTEAD

ST. PANCRAS

ISLINGTON

HACKNEY

8

WEST HAM

EAST HAM

BARKING

UXBRIDGE

WILLESDEN

5

9

POPLAR

HAYES & HARLINGTON

EALING

ACTON

KENSINGTON

HAMMERSMITH

CITY

STEPNEY

6

1

SOUTHALL

10

2

7

BERMONDSEY

WOOLWICH

ERITH

YIEWSLEY & W. DRAYTON

HESTON & ISLEWORTH

11

FULHAM

BATTERSEA

LAMBETH

DEPTFORD

GREENWICH

STAINES

BARNES

WANDSWORTH

CAMBERWELL

BEXLEY

CRAYFORD

FELTHAM

RICHMOND

LEWISHAM

CHISLEHURST & SIDCUP

TWICKENHAM

MALDEN & COOMBE

WIMBLEDON

14

BECKENHAM

SUNBURY ON THAMES

13

MERTON & MORDEN

MITCHAM

BEDDINGTON & WALLINGTON

BROMLEY

SURBITON

SUTTON & CHEAM

CARSHALTON

CROYDON

ORPINGTON

ESHER

EPSOM & EWELL

COULSDON & PURLEY

BANSTEAD

1   BETHNAL GREEN
2   CHELSEA
3   FINSBURY
4   HOLBORN
5   PADDINGTON

6   SHOREDITCH
7   SOUTHWARK
8   STOKE NEWINGTON
9   ST. MARYLEBONE
10   WESTMINSTER

11   BRENTFORD & CHISWICK
12   FRIERN BARNET
13   KINGSTON-ON-THAMES
14   PENGE

KEY MAP
GREATER LONDON AREAS   (1951)

THE INDUSTRIES OF LONDON

GEOGRAPHY

Editors

PROFESSOR S. W. WOOLDRIDGE, C.B.E., D.SC., F.R.S.

and

PROFESSOR W. G. EAST, M.A.

Professors of Geography in the University of London

A.V.H.

B.H.

THE INDUSTRIES
OF LONDON

Since 1861

P. G. HALL

Lecturer in Geography, Birkbeck College,
University of London

HUTCHINSON UNIVERSITY LIBRARY

LONDON

HUTCHINSON & CO. (*Publishers*) LTD
178–202 Great Portland Street, London, W.1

London Melbourne Sydney
Auckland Bombay Toronto
Johannesburg New York

★

First published 1962

CONTENTS

LIST OF MAPS

ACKNOWLEDGMENTS

First I want to thank the staffs of the University Library in Cambridge and the British Museum for their constant service and expert advice while I gathered the material for this book. I owe an especial debt to the staffs of the Official Publications Department in Cambridge and of the State Paper Room and Map Room at the Museum. Chapter 13 could not have been written without the help of officials of the Ministry of Labour Statistical Department at Watford, for which I am most grateful. Birkbeck College has provided what is for me the happiest of all academic environments in which to write the book. Within the College my particular thanks go to Miss Pamela Balfry, who typed the manuscript, and to Mrs Marian Schofield, who drew most of the maps.

The following people have kindly given me permission to reproduce material, mine or theirs: the Council of the Institute of British Geographers, for material on the clothing trades first published in the *Transactions* of the Institute; and Mr B. A. Bates, for material of his which appears in Chapter 8. I am indebted to Mr Bates for reading and criticizing Chapter 8 in draft, and to Mr John Hall for reading the whole manuscript and for making valuable comments on it. Finally I owe a very particular debt to Professor W. G. East, who as joint editor of the series has read the manuscript at successive stages and has given most freely of advice and encouragement.

P. G. H.

NOTE

1. Areas. Throughout this book reference is made to the pattern of administrative areas which existed at the time of writing (February 1961). The 'County of London' refers to the area of the London County Council, comprising the City of London and the 28 metropolitan boroughs, as created by the Acts of 1888 and 1899. Following the recommendations of the Royal Commission on Local Government in Greater London in 1960, it seems likely that legislation will be introduced to replace the present pattern by a Greater London Council covering the whole of the Greater London conurbation, and a new pattern of Greater London boroughs. Those who may read this book when the new system has come into being should bear this in mind.

2. Footnotes. The following abbreviations are used throughout the footnotes:

    P.P.   British Parliamentary Papers

    R.C.   Royal Commission

    S.C.   Select Committee

I

INTRODUCTION

> Comparisons with the past are absolutely necessary to the
> true comprehension of all that exists to-day; without them
> we cannot penetrate to the heart of things.
>
> Charles Booth: *Life and Labour of the*
> *People in London*, 3rd ed., final vol., p. 31

THIS book is a study in economic geography, treated historically.
Its primary purpose is to describe and explain the industrial
geography of London at the present time, using the most recent
statistics available for that purpose. Even the broad features of the
present-day pattern will be unfamiliar to many, and this fact alone
provides some justification for the present book. But, as is commonly
the case with the geography of a complex economic unit, the present
makes no sense until it is related to the evolutionary process which
has produced it. The problem arises: how far is it necessary to go
back into the past, to provide adequate explanation of the present?
Here the answer is that detailed study of the structure of industry
should be carried back for about a century. The precise date chosen,
1861, is significant because here the statistical data become adequate
for detailed study of industrial geography.

The picture thus revealed may be surprising to many, who may
share the view put forward by the author of one of the innumerable
guides to London published for the visitor to the Great Exhibition
in 1851:

> Our large manufacturing districts are, for obvious reasons,
> located in the vicinity of our coal-fields. . . . London may be
> regarded as a vast trading and commercial, rather than a manu-
> facturing town, and hence, from the great subdivision of em-
> ployments, and the multiplicity of objects to be noticed, it is
> much more difficult to convey a general, and at the same time

9

an accurate idea of the useful arts and trades carried on in this great city, than it would be to describe the industry of a town devoted to large and important manufactures.[1]

The wide currency which such a view has obtained may be judged by the fact that nearly 100 years after this was written the Greater London Plan of 1944 could describe London as '*now* the country's most important manufacturing centre', following 'phenomenal increase in . . . industrialisation' since 1918.[2] In fact, London was the chief manufacturing centre of the country in 1861, and without doubt for centuries before that. The industries which contributed to this importance gave mid-Victorian London a clearly-defined manufacturing structure, even though this structure was much more complex than that of Lancashire or the West Riding. One purpose of this book is to describe this structure in detail, and to show how it was overlain gradually by a new structure resulting from technological developments in the late nineteenth and early twentieth centuries.

The industry of London is a vast subject, and to study it adequately is beyond the capacity of any one man. Up to now only isolated studies of certain aspects have existed.[3] This book does not pretend to be a comprehensive study, but a preliminary essay on the subject. One day, it is to be hoped, it will be complemented by a detailed work based necessarily upon co-operative effort. Its limitations will soon be apparent to the reader. Apart from brief references in Chapters 3 and 13 to service industries, it is limited to manufacturing industries, and thus excludes the analysis of the industries which many people think most characteristic of a large metropolis—distributive trades, banking, insurance, administration, professional and personal services of all sorts. Within the manufacturing industries this study concentrates most heavily on the trades which were already firmly established in mid-nineteenth-century London. This has been done deliberately, in order to correct the misapprehensions described above. For the newer industries it draws in part upon the work of others, some unpublished, some long out of print.

The plan of the book is simple. Chapter 2 is technical. It discusses the sources of information available for the study of industrial geography in this country on a statistical basis; their limitations, and methods of overcoming these, at least in part; and ways of presenting the material thus obtained. The chapter should chiefly interest research workers in industrial geography, though for reasons of space it cannot pretend to be an adequate treatment of the problems involved. General readers may prefer to avoid it, except for the essential explanation of statistical terms on pages 16–17. Chapter 3 then presents a broad survey of the main types of industry—primary, manufacturing and service—and their distribution within London, and goes on to pick out the most important individual manufacturing industries of London. On this basis, Chapters 4–6 then discuss some older-established industries and Chapter 7 draws certain general conclusions about them. In Chapter 8 the historical development of the newer industrial areas of outer London is described. Chapters 9–11 describe three of the most important newer industries. In Chapter 12 an attempt is made to compare and contrast what has been learned about the older and the newer industries, and to relate them to the gradual pattern of historical evolution. Finally, Chapter 13 assesses the effect of planning policy on London industry since 1940.

London in this book means Greater London, that is the area roughly coterminous with the Metropolitan Police District, and bounded roughly by a circle of radius 15 miles from Charing Cross. This area consists of 721·6 square miles—1·24 per cent of the area of England and Wales. It extends to Waltham Holy Cross in the north-east, to Orpington in the south-east, to Esher in the south-west and nearly (but not quite) to Watford in the north-west. Since 1951 there is powerful evidence that this area is becoming inadequate as a definition of London.[4] But for a study whose main statistical terminus is 1951 it is just adequate.

1   John Weale (ed.), *London exhibited in 1851* (1851), 220.
2   L.P. Abercrombie, *Greater London Plan 1944* (H.M.S.O. 1945), 39; my italics.
3   The most important are: D. H. Smith, *The Industries of Greater London* (1933); O. H. K. Spate, 'Geographical Aspects of the Industrial Evolution of London till 1850', *Geographical Journal*, 92 (1938), 422–32; M. J. Wise, 'The Role of London in the Industrial Geography of Great Britain', *Geography*, 41 (1956), 219–32; R. C. Estall and J. E. Martin, 'Industry in Greater London', *Town Planning Review*, 28 (1957–8), 261–77.
4   A. G. Powell, 'The Recent Development of Greater London', *The Advancement of Science*, 17 (1960–1), 76–86.

SOURCE MATERIALS AND
THEIR PROBLEMS

THERE is no single statistical source which will measure reliably and in detail the changing industrial geography of Britain over the last hundred years. Instead, there are a number of partly unsatisfactory sources, each with its own individual defects.

Minor sources

Certain sources may be regarded as minor ones, because they do not exist either for a sufficiently long historical period, or in sufficient geographical detail, or both. There are four of these.

1. *Ministry of Labour Employment Statistics*.[1] These cover a wide range of industries and are available for every year after 1920. They were based on a standard classification from 1923 onwards, and are thus comparable only from 1923 to 1948, when a new run began. And until 1948 they did not cover all workers. For these reasons the Ministry of Labour statistics are unsatisfactory for the purpose of this book. Post-1948 statistics are, however, used in Chapter 13 to measure changes which have occurred since the 1951 Census.

2. *Census of Production*. The Board of Trade has taken a full Census of Production at irregular intervals during this century, for the years 1907, 1912, 1924, 1930, 1935, 1948, 1949, 1950, 1951, 1954 and 1958.[2] The most important information given in the Census Reports is that about output (in terms of quantity and value); employment; cost of materials; power and fuel used; and (in some Censuses since 1948) patterns of sales. Unfortunately the Census has never gone into great geographical detail. Most of the statistics have referred to the whole of England and Wales or the entire United Kingdom. In a few Censuses there has been an analysis into Administrative Divisions, but this is insufficient for the purpose of this book. Further, since 1930 most of the information given has been restricted to large establishments, employing more than 10

persons. This seriously vitiates the use of Census materials for industries where there are many small firms, as with many important London industries. Lastly, a rule against disclosure of information about individual firms has led in many cases to the complete omission of statistics where an industry is dominated by a single large firm. For these reasons the Census of Production is used here only as a supplementary, interpretative source, to provide information about factors of location such as the use of mechanical power, or the ways in which the final product is disposed of. It cannot serve as a basic source.

3. *Surveys of Industrial Development*. These also were produced by the Board of Trade, for the years 1933–8 inclusive.[3] Each survey gives detailed particulars of factories opened, extended or transferred during the year. Because they cover such a short span of time, the Surveys cannot serve as a basic source. But for the rapidly-changing industrial geography of Britain during the 1930's they are a special source of unique value.

4. *Factory Inspectors' Records*. The unpublished Home Office Factory Inspectors' Records provide a source of great value for the detailed mapping of the present industrial geography of Britain. But they are not available in comprehensive form far enough backwards in time to serve as a statistical basis for the present work. And their bulk and complexity have so far precluded comprehensive analysis covering the whole of Greater London, even for a single date, though there are hopes that this will be achieved in time.

The Census: comparison of occupations[4]

The first main source is the decennial Census of Population. Every edition of the Census since 1801 has included occupational tables in some form for administrative areas within the United Kingdom, which might provide a source for a study of changing industrial location based on numbers employed.

Up to the present time surprisingly few research workers have tried to discover how far the different classifications of occupations, used at successive Censuses, can be made comparable; these few have often emerged critical of Census methods.[5] The Census authorities themselves have attempted comparisons very seldom, and seem to have underestimated the difficulties involved.[6] The discussion here must be restricted to changes since 1861.

The most important change that has occurred in classification since 1861 is the division (since 1911 and on a full scale since 1921) into separate and parallel 'Occupational' and 'Industrial' classifications. A typist in an engineering works is classified under clerical work in the Occupational Classification, but under engineering in the Industrial Classification. The first relates to the nature of the occupation, the second to the end-product of the work. An Industrial Classification is the relevant one for the present purpose. The one used as basis for comparisons here is the Industrial Classification of the 1951 Census, which is based on the Standard Industrial Classification introduced in 1948.

Earlier Census classifications must therefore be reshuffled to accord with the 1951 groupings. Here the 1861 Census presents least difficulty. It is mainly industrial rather than occupational in nature.[7] It also gives extremely detailed information for relatively small administrative areas, corresponding roughly to the present metropolitan boroughs of London, and so permits reasonably accurate reclassification under the 1951 headings. The 1861 classification is used as the statistical starting-point of this book, to provide a picture of the mid-Victorian distribution of industry in London.

Between 1871 and 1921 the surprising fact is that no Census contains sufficient local detail within London for a satisfactory picture of the industrial geography. In addition, between 1881 and 1911 the basis of classification is an occupational one, and so is comparable neither with earlier classifications nor with the later industrial classifications. The 1921 Census does, however, provide modern industrial statistics for Greater London as a whole, and these are very useful because they show the state of industrial development in London at an important stage, just before the great expansion of the interwar years.

The 1931 industrial statistics are set out in great local detail for administrative areas within Greater London, but unfortunately they relate to place of residence. By 1931 the increasing divergence in London between home and work had made place-of-residence statistics of very little use to the student of industrial location. The 1951 statistics rectified this error.

The inevitable conclusion is that, for detailed study within Greater London, the only comparison which may be safely made is for the years 1861 and 1951. For England and Wales, and for Greater London as a whole, the 1921 Census is also available.

There are certain official and semi-official guides to the changes which have occurred, which are essential to research workers in this field.[8] They are especially helpful in dealing with the very complex transfers which came about with the change from an industrial to an occupational basis in 1881, and back again to the modern industrial basis in 1911–21. In some cases these changes were so radical that no precise historical comparison is possible: engineering is an example. But for many important London trades, like clothing, the problems can be surmounted.

There are in addition large general problems of comparison between Census and Census. In 1861 the detailed statistics for local areas apply only to persons of 20 years and upwards. This limitation excludes a much larger part of the total labour force in some occupations (e.g. dressmaking) than in others (e.g. medicine). The figure for each Census group or unit in each area therefore has to be inflated by a ratio derived from a larger area (corresponding to the present County of London), for which figures were also given for workers of less than 20. In 1921 the lower age limit was 14 and in 1951 15, the school-leaving age. The 1861 Census put retired people and the inmates of institutions under their former occupations; after 1881 they were classed as unoccupied. This change probably did not affect more than about 2 per cent of the employed population.[9] The form of the schedule was progressively improved so that the numbers in indeterminate general classes, such as labourers, declined.

The largest general problem is, however, that only the 1921 and 1951 Industry Tables refer to place of work. It has already been noted that the 1931 Industry Tables are invalidated because they refer to place of residence. The mid-Victorian Censuses have the same fault, but it was not such a grievous one then, because people lived much nearer their work, and this applied especially to the manufacturing workers who were often employed casually. There is no statistical evidence for Victorian times of the relation between work and residence save for the inadequate City of London Day Censuses of 1866, 1881, 1891 and 1911.[10] But there is plenty of contemporary evidence from reliable witnesses.[11] The 1861 Censuses may therefore be used as a reliable source for the distribution of industry in Victorian London.

The Census: statistical techniques

The processing of the Census statistics makes easier direct comparisons from date to date, and avoids difficulties arising from general changes in the treatment of the retired after 1881.

The statistical measures used here are based on those devised by P. Sargant Florence.[12] Florence's first index is called the *Location Quotient* (L.Q.). It measures the degree to which a particular industry is concentrated in a particular region of the country (*vis-à-vis* the whole country), compared with the extent to which all the country's industry is concentrated in that region. Using a criterion of workers employed, the Quotient for (say) clothing would thus be obtained from the formula:

$$\frac{\text{Numbers employed in clothing in the region, as a percentage of the national total}}{\text{Numbers employed in all industries in the region, as a percentage of the national total}}$$

Thus Greater London in 1861 is found to have had 15·6 per cent of all the workers in the country, but 22·4 per cent of the clothing workers; so its L.Q. for clothing at that date was 22·4 divided by 15·6, or 1·4.

Florence's second index, the *Coefficient of Localization* (C.L.), expresses in a single figure the degree to which a particular industry is localized or dispersed within all the regions of the country. In Florence's words:

When workers are divided up region by region as percentages of the total in all regions, the coefficient is the sum (divided by 100) of the plus deviations of the regional percentages of workers in the particular industry from the corresponding regional percentages of workers in all industry. Complete coincidence, region by region, of the particular industry with all industry gives a coefficient of 0, extreme differentiation (e.g. workers in the particular industry being all concentrated in one region) gives a figure approaching 1.[13]

The Location Quotient for Greater London is used in this book, but not the Coefficient of Localization. Chief use is made of two indices derived respectively from the Quotient and the Coefficient. They are called the *Local Location Quotient* (L.L.Q.) and the *Coefficient of Local Concentration* (C.L.C.). In them, the base of comparison is not the national total of workers, but the total for Greater London. Against this base is measured the degree of concentration, not among relatively large regions of the country, but among the small administrative areas within the bounds of Greater London. For example, Westminster in 1861 had 9·3 per cent of all the workers in Greater London, but 18·5 per cent of its tailors; so its L.L.Q. for tailoring was 18·5 divided by 9·3, or 2·0.

The Census: comparison of areas

The problem of comparison of areas is altogether simpler. The changes have been less complex, and the problems they present are more readily overcome. The 1861 occupational tables refer to Registration Districts. These, the fundamental units of nineteenth-century Census enumeration, were created by the Births and Deaths Registration Act of 1836, and in turn were based on the unions of parishes established by the Poor Law Amendment Act of 1834. By the 1901 Census they had been completely superseded by the modern pattern of Local Government Areas established by the Public Health Act of 1872, the Local Government Act of 1888 and the London Government Act of 1899.[14]

The problem is to fit the older Registration Districts to today's scheme of Local Government Areas. Thus in 1861 no precise occupational figures can be obtained for the entire Greater London area, whose outer boundary by no means corresponds with the boundaries of the then Registration Districts. The occupational figures for these Districts have therefore had to be reduced by fixed ratios derived from their total populations and the populations of those parts within Greater London. The arbitrary element in this is not serious because at that time there were relatively few manufacturing or service workers in these outer areas.

Directories

The second main statistical source is the information in the Post Office London Directory and the associated directories for the London suburbs. With them the central problem is how to define industries and trades, in order to compare them from one date to another. Here the crux is to distinguish manufacturing from selling elements. A second problem with the Directory material is that it cannot be processed to obtain an index of localization, as can the Census figures, since there is no total of industrial units to compare with the number in a particular industry, whether for London as a whole or for individual administrative areas within it. The Directory material used here is therefore mapped unprocessed, in the form of simple dot distributions. Because of this, and because of the associated difficulty that the entries do not distinguish firms of different sizes, the Directory material can provide no consistent measure of actual industrial activity. It cannot serve as a central index, but merely as supplementary material about the detailed distribution of industry in small areas of concentration, and the changes in these distributions in time.

1   *Guides to Official Sources*, no. 1, *Labour Statistics* (H.M.S.O. 1958), 2–4, 7–8; R. B. Ainsworth, 'United Kingdom Labour Statistics', *Journal of the Royal Statistical Society*, series A, 113 (1950), 37–49.

2   H.M.S.O. 1907 in the *P.P.* series: 1909, CII; 1910, CIX; 1911, CI; 1912–13, CIX. The rest separately.

3   Board of Trade, *Survey of Industrial Development*, annual parts (H.M.S.O. 1934–9).

4   *Guides to Official Sources*, no. 2, *Census Reports of Great Britain 1801–1931* (H.M.S.O. 1951), 27–65.

5   C. Booth, 'Occupations of the People of the United Kingdom, 1801–81', *Journal of the Statistical Society*, 49 (1886), 318; and P. Sargant Florence, 'The Selection of Industries suitable for dispersion into Rural Areas', *Journal of the Royal Statistical Society*, 107 (1944), 115. The most recent attempt at comparison is Joyce Bellamy, 'Occupations in Kingston-upon-Hull, 1841–1948', *Yorkshire Bulletin of Economic and Social Research*, 4 (1952), 33–50.

6   See *Census 1951. Classification of Industries* (H.M.S.O. 1952), iv, where it is claimed that the 1951 classification is 'largely comparable' with that of 1931, though there are detailed and complex changes.

7   *Instructions for the Use of the Clerks employed in classifying the Occupations and Ages of the People. . . .* (H.M.S.O. 1862), 6.

8   For 1871–81–91: Return in *P.P.* 1895, LXXX. For 1891–1901–1911:
    Census 1911, summary tables 63 and 64; *P.P.* 1914–16, LXXXI. For
    1911 Occupational-Industrial: ibid., table 66. For 1911–21: A. L.
    Bowley, 'Numbers Occupied in the Industries of England and Wales,
    1911 and 1921', *London and Cambridge Economic Service, Special
    Memorandum*, no. 17A (1926).

9   *Census 1881, General Report*, 28, *P.P.* 1883, LXXX.

10 1866 apparently did not exist as a separate publication. 1881 and 1891
    were issued by the Local Government and Taxation Committee of
    the City Council; 1911 by the County Purposes Committee.

11 See G. A. Sekon, *Locomotion in Victorian London* (1938), 8; J. H.
    Clapham in G. M. Young (ed.), *Early Victorian England 1830–1865*
    (1934), I, 22; R. H. Mottram, ibid., I, 172–3; *R. C. Housing Working
    Classes*, Q. 739, *P.P.* 1884–5, XXX.

12 P. Sargant Florence, *Investment, Location, and Size of Plant* (National
    Institute of Economic and Social Research: Economic and Social
    Studies, 7, Cambridge 1948), 34–7, 41 n. The Quotient has also been
    called the Index of Specialization. C. J. Robertson, 'Locational and
    Structural Aspects of Industry in Edinburgh', *Scottish Geographical
    Magazine*, 74 (1958), 65–77, and the references there given.

13 Florence, ibid., 34. The statistical difficulties involved in use of the
    coefficient are examined in Florence, J.R.S.S. 1944, op. cit., 111, 116.
    See also the index devised by C. Day, 'The Distribution of Industrial
    Occupations in England, 1841–1861', *Transactions of the Connecticut
    Academy of Arts and Sciences*, 28 (1927), especially 202–21.

14 V. D. Lipman, *Local Government Areas, 1834–1945* (1945), chapters
    I–IV; Guides to Census Reports, op. cit., 95–104; W. A. Robson, *The
    Government and Misgovernment of London* (1948), chapters IX, X.

3

THE INDUSTRIAL STRUCTURE OF LONDON

THIS chapter gives a broad description of the structure of employment in London and the ways in which it has changed over the last hundred years. More particularly, it tries to answer three of the four questions which are central to the theme of this book.

The first two questions are about the pattern of employment in Greater London as a whole, *vis-à-vis* England and Wales.

1. How important, relatively, in Greater London are the three main types of employment—primary, manufacturing and service?

2. What are the most important individual employment groups within London, in terms of the 1951 Industrial Classification?

The statistical answers to these questions are expressed as percentages of total employment and as Location Quotients for Greater London.* They are based on the statistics set out in the Appendix, which represent the result of the reclassification of the 1861 and 1921 statistics to the 1951 base.

The third and fourth questions are about the geographical pattern of industry *within* Greater London.

3. What is the distribution within Greater London of workers in the three main employment types—primary, manufacturing and service?

4. What is the distribution of the most important individual employment groups within London? This question is not answered in this chapter but throughout the rest of the book.

The statistical answers to these questions are expressed as percentages of Greater London totals, Local Location Quotients and Coefficients of Local Concentration.*

* For explanation of these terms see pp. 16–17.

Three main types of employment

Table 1 below has been produced from statistics in the Appendix in order to show the facts about the three main types of employment.

TABLE 1

THREE MAIN TYPES OF EMPLOYMENT: ENGLAND AND WALES, GREATER LONDON, 1861, 1921, 1951

(Source: Censuses, 1861, 1921, 1951)

Total employed (thousands)

	England and Wales			Greater London		
	1861	*1921*	*1951*	*1861*	*1921*	*1951*
Primary	2276·9	2395·9	1705·2	44·0	29·0	19·8
Manufacturing	3149·9	5979·9	7532·8	468·8	1052·6	1522·5
Service	3719·9	8414·1	10685·0	903·0	2089·5	2741·5
Not stated	346·3	388·2	17·0	63·0	45·0	4·5
Total employed	9493·0	17178·0	19940·0	1478·8	3216·1	4288·3

Percentage of total employed

	England and Wales			Greater London		
	1861	*1921*	*1951*	*1861*	*1921*	*1951*
Primary	24·0	13·9	8·6	3·0	0·9	0·5
Manufacturing	33·2	34·8	37·8	31·7	32·7	35·5
Service	39·2	49·0	53·6	61·0	65·0	63·9
Not stated	3·7	2·2	0·1	4·3	1·4	0·1
Total employed	100·0	100·0	100·0	100·0	100·0	100·0

	Greater London per cent of England and Wales			Greater London Location Quotient		
	1861	*1921*	*1951*	*1861*	*1921*	*1951*
Primary	1·9	1·2	1·2	0·12	0·07	0·05
Manufacturing	14·9	17·6	20·2	0·96	0·94	0·94
Service	24·3	24·8	25·7	1·56	1·33	1·19
Total employed	15·6	18·7	21·5	1·00	1·00	1·00

(Totals may not exactly agree due to rounding)

TABLE 1—(contd.)

	Average annual rate of change (plus unless indicated)			
	England and Wales		Greater London	
	1861–1921	1921–1951	1861–1921	1921–1951
Primary	0·1	—0·9	—0·5	—0·9
Manufacturing	1·0	0·8	1·4	1·3
Service	1·4	0·8	1·4	0·9
Total employed	1·0	0·5	1·3	0·9

This table brings out certain important facts. First, during the last hundred years London has been the most important single centre of economic activity in the country, in terms of numbers employed. Were statistics available they would doubtless show that this has been the case for a thousand years or more. In 1861 London contained between one in six and one in seven of all the workers in England and Wales; in 1921, between one in five and one in six; in 1951, over one in five. If there were available for the period other indices of economic activity, such as value of product, they would without doubt tell the same story.

Secondly, there are large differences in the degree to which the three main industrial types have been concentrated in the capital. In primary industry—agriculture, fishing, mining and quarrying—London has always had a negligible share of the country's total employment: just under 2 per cent in 1861, just over 1 per cent in 1951. With a limited and progressively diminishing agricultural area, and with negligible resources for extractive industry (apart from a little brick clay or gravel, now largely worked out or built over), these proportions are not surprising.

Manufacturing industry as defined here comprises Orders III–XVI, inclusive, of the 1951 Industrial Classification. It excludes building and contracting and the public utility industries of gas, water and electricity supply. As thus defined, at each of the three dates chosen, manufacturing workers were concentrated in Greater London to almost exactly the same extent as were all workers. At all three dates the capital was clearly the most important single seat of manufacturing industry in the country, accounting for between one and six and one in seven of all manufacturing workers in 1861, over one in six in 1921, and over one in five in 1951. Manufacturing occupied nearly one in three of all workers in London in 1861, over one in three in 1951. These are important and striking facts. They flatly deny the traditional assumption about London, implicitly underlying many of the references to it in economic geographies or economic histories, that it came into existence as a major manufacturing centre after the turn of this century, perhaps even after 1918. In fact, Victorian London had a large and varied manufacturing industry, on which the present industrial structure was built.

The definition of service industry used here comprises the items XVII–XXIV, inclusive, of the 1951 Industrial Classification, including building and contracting, public utilities, transport, distribution, finance, administration, professional services and miscellaneous services. The table shows that during the period 1861–1951 workers in service industries as thus defined have consistently made up just over three-fifths of the total labour force of London, and that London has accounted consistently for about a quarter of all the service workers of England and Wales. Both in the entire country and in London the service trades have increased rapidly in employment during the 90-year period. As the importance of manufacturing in London has risen, the Location Quotient for the services has, however, fallen correspondingly, from 1·6 in 1861 to 1·2 in 1951.

Leading industrial groups

The second question asks which industrial groups (in terms of 1951 Industrial Orders and selected headings) have been and are most important in London. Here it is important to realize that there are two senses in which an industry may be important in the economy of an area. The more obvious sense is that the industry has a large share of the total economic activity of the area, as measured here by numbers of workers. The other sense is that the industry (whether important or not in the first sense) is exceptionally concentrated in the area *vis-à-vis* a bigger area (e.g. the whole country) of which it forms a part. Importance in this latter sense is measured by the Location Quotient.

On the basis of this distinction Table 2 below shows industrial groups in order of their importance in Greater London in 1861 and 1951.

TABLE 2

LEADING INDUSTRIAL GROUPS:
GREATER LONDON, 1861 AND 1951

(Source: Censuses, 1861 and 1951)

A Order in terms of percentage of total workers

	1861	per cent		1951	per cent
1	Miscellaneous services	25·2	1	Distributive trades	14·0
2	Clothing	13·3	2	Miscellaneous services	11·3
3	Distributive trades	9·4	3	Professional services	8·5
4	Building	6·6	4	Building	6·6
5	Professional services	5·0	5	National administration	4·5
6	Agriculture, fishing	2·9	6	Insurance, banking and finance	4·4
7	Water, dock transport	2·8	7 {	Clothing	4·3
				Electrical engineering	4·3
8	Road transport	2·7	9	General engineering	3·8
9	Communications, other transport	2·6			
10 {	National administration	2·3	10	Vehicles	3·4
	Insurance, banking and finance	2·3			

B Order in terms of Location Quotient

	1861	L.Q.		1951	L.Q.
1	Paint	5·2	1	Air transport	3·2
2	Rubber	4·3	2	Precision instruments	2·3
3	Tobacco	4·0	3	Insurance, banking and finance	2·2
4	Printing	3·4	4	Printing	2·0
5	Paper products	3·0	5	Other manufacturing	1·9
6	Precision instruments	2·6	6 {	Furniture	1·8
7	Furniture	2·5		Leather goods	1·8
8	Communications, other transport	2·4		Paint	1·8
9 {	Gas, water	2·2	9	Communications, other transport	1·7
	Insurance, banking and finance	2·2	10 {	Electrical engineering	1·6
				Paper products	1·6

The 42 places in this table are in fact filled by 25 industries. One of these (agriculture in 1861) is primary; 13 are manufacturing; and 11 are service industries.

Of the manufacturing industries, seven appear twice. Clothing appears twice on account of percentage importance. Paint, precision instruments, furniture, paper products and printing each appear twice because of their high London L.Q.s; these are the smaller London trades that for one reason or another are exceptionally concentrated in the metropolis. Lastly, electrical engineering, which did not exist as an industry in 1861, appeared in 1951 both on the grounds of percentage and L.Q.

It is extremely significant that this last combination is a rare one in London manufacturing. Certain manufactures do stand out, but less clearly so than do certain manufactures in other great manufacturing districts. As Ernest Aves put it in the Booth Survey of the 90's, 'London has no single staple industry'.[1] There is no industry like Lancashire cotton, which has both a large percentage of all the workers in the area, and a large percentage of all the workers in that industry in the country.[2] The most important industries on the basis of percentages also have L.Q.s above unity, but the latter are not exceptionally high; they do not exceed 2·5. Conversely, the industries that do have high L.Q.s in London are small trades like precision instruments, or paint and rubber in 1861.

This complex character of London's manufacturing structures is, of course, a natural corollary of its immense size. Lancashire's industry is more homogeneous partly because it has a smaller total of workers; the smaller the economic unit the greater the possible homogeneity. As a nineteenth-century observer said:

> Large provincial towns, such as Leeds and Sheffield, stand out distinctly in the manufacturing scenery of England. . . . Perhaps this is clearer from the fact of their being characterised by special manufactures, such as woollen cloth and cutlery; still their prominence is partly due to their distinctiveness. Were they suburbs of London the case might be somewhat different.[3]

The 'great subdivision of employments, and the multiplicity of objects' was a good reason for the failure of nineteenth-century observers to appreciate the importance of London manufacturing.

Almost every manufacturing industry in Table 2 has a lower Location Quotient in 1951 than in 1861. This is characteristic of a tendency, not only for Greater London but for all the regions of the country, to approach more closely in industrial structure to the national average. The same process was noticed by Wilfred Smith for Merseyside.[4]

The second question has an important corollary. Are there any manufactures relatively important in the national industrial structure, but unimportant in London's? There are two such: metal manufacture and textiles. The metals group, Order V of the 1951 Census, comprises the smelting, converting, refining and rolling of iron and steel; founding; the manufacture of steel sheets and tinplate and of iron and steel tubes; and the smelting and refining of non-ferrous metals. These branches use great quantities of coal and raw materials, and came in the nineteenth century to be located on the major coalfields, where by and large they have remained.

TABLE 3

METAL MANUFACTURE AND TEXTILES:

ENGLAND AND WALES, GREATER LONDON, 1861, 1921, 1951

(Source: Censuses, 1861, 1921, 1951)

	Metal manufacture			Textiles		
	1861	*1921*	*1951*	*1861*	*1921*	*1951*
Percentage of total employed:						
In England and Wales	1·6	2·3	2·5	10·6	6·7	4·4
In Greater London	0·4	0·4	0·6	1·9	0·7	0·6
Greater London per cent } *England and Wales*	3·7	3·1	4·9	2·8	2·0	3·1
Greater London L.Q.	0·2	0·2	0·2	0·2	0·1	0·1

Textiles are an even more extreme case. Save for the now-decayed Spitalfields silk industry, the main textile industries also came during the Industrial Revolution to be situated near coal, and industrial inertia has since kept them there. There has been a slight increase in London's share since 1921, based on the manufacture of artificial fibres, but it is of small importance.

It is notable that manufacturing industries which represent

earlier links in the productive process are less important in London than those representing later links. Thus London is deficient in textiles, not in clothing; in woodworking, not in furniture; in paper production, not in stationery or printing. This pattern is characteristic of a major market centre.

Of the 11 service industries which appear in the order-of-importance table, one (banking, insurance and finance) appears four times, one (communications) three times, and five (building and contracting, distribution, national administration, professional services and miscellaneous services) twice. Communications qualifies at both dates on L.Q., and in 1861 on percentage. The five services appearing twice do so on the basis of percentage importance alone. The most important of these are miscellaneous services and distributive trades, which together accounted for nearly three-fifths of total employment in the service trades in 1861, and nearly two-fifths in 1951. These are trades which are important in London because they are important everywhere. Of course, service industries more commonly have this characteristic than do manufacturing industries; their L.Q.s are usually lower, because a large part of service employment is apt to be engaged in providing services for the local population.

There is only one service industry which was important in the national economy but less in London's: rail transport, which had a Location Quotient below unity in 1861, barely above unity in 1951. This industry came in the nineteenth century to be concentrated to an exceptional degree in 'company towns', built by the railway companies around their workshops at provincial junctions. Only the Great Eastern, at Stratford, created a true railway town within the Greater London area, and this was not large enough to affect the general picture. The development of the underground railways in this century has undoubtedly been the chief factor in the increased concentration of railway workers recorded in 1951.

All the other service trades were at the dates chosen relatively more important in London than in the country as a whole, often substantially more so. This was so because of London's centuries-old functions of political capital, chief social centre and leading port of a nation which was the first in Europe to achieve real unity, and later the first to engage on a large scale in world trade. The concentration of the service trades in London is to be explained therefore in the first place by reference to the historical development of these varied functions, which is undertaken in Chapter 7.

Geography of the three main types of employment

The third question concerns the geography within the Greater London area of the three main employment groups—primary, manufacturing and service.

Primary industry is not of great importance in Greater London. It has concentrated in the outer parts of the area and has progressively retreated outwards in the face of competing land uses which employ the land more intensively and so can afford to pay more for it. The most important primary industry, and the greatest loser, has, of course, been agriculture (including fishing) which accounted for nearly 99 per cent of all workers in primary industry in 1861 and about 86 per cent in 1951.[5]

Manufacturing industry embraces a great variety of trades, which might be expected to show very different patterns of location. Despite this fact, manufacturing industry as a whole has a clear pattern of distribution within Greater London. The pattern of distribution may be considered in absolute terms (numbers of workers) or relative terms (measured by high Local Location Quotients). In Figures 1 and 2 both these criteria are used. The qualification for inclusion is either 23,000 workers or a L.L.Q. of 1·2.

The 1861 statistics present a simple case. Eight areas, or just over one-fifth of all the areas separately distinguished at that date, contained 261,000 workers or 56 per cent of the manufacturing workers of Greater London. All but two of these had Local Location Quotients above unity. The two exceptions were Westminster and St Marylebone, making up the manufacturing area of the West End. Though there were great numbers of manufacturing workers there, relatively they were outweighed by the workers in the service industries. No area other than those listed had a L.L.Q. above 1·2 in 1861. Figure 1 shows that the eight areas were concentrated in a sector of the present-day County of London, running from the central districts of Westminster and the City (and stretching south of the river into Southwark), towards the northern and eastern boundaries of the county. This sector was, however, broken into two separate projections by the blank areas of Holborn, the City

and Islington, which at that date contained relatively few manufacturing workers. The break emphasized the distinction between
two independent centres, one in the East End and Southwark, the
other in the West End. The horseshoe-shaped belt thus formed was
the great zone of manufacturing industry in mid-Victorian London.

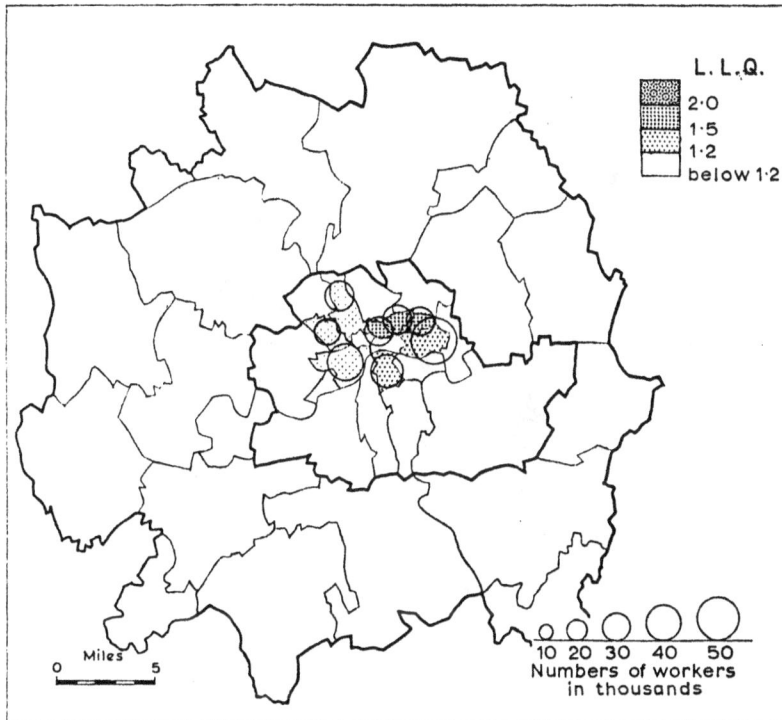

Fig. 1. Greater London: manufacturing industry, 1861 (Source: Census
1861. Boundaries in Outer Ring are 1861 Registration Districts)

The 1951 statistics present a more complicated picture. There
were then 26 areas with more than 23,000 manufacturing workers in
each—just over a quarter of all the administrative areas in Greater
London. Together these accounted for 973,000 workers—nearly
64 per cent of the manufacturing workers of Greater London, as
compared with 56 per cent in 1861. But in addition there were
20 smaller concentrations of manufacturing workers with high
L.L.Q.s for manufacturing (1·2 or more). Together these areas

accounted for another 234,000 workers or 15 per cent of the Greater
London total. So, in all, on the basis of the chosen criteria, in 1861
just over one-fifth of the various areas of London contained just
over half the manufacturing workers; in 1951 almost half the areas
contained almost exactly four-fifths of the workers.

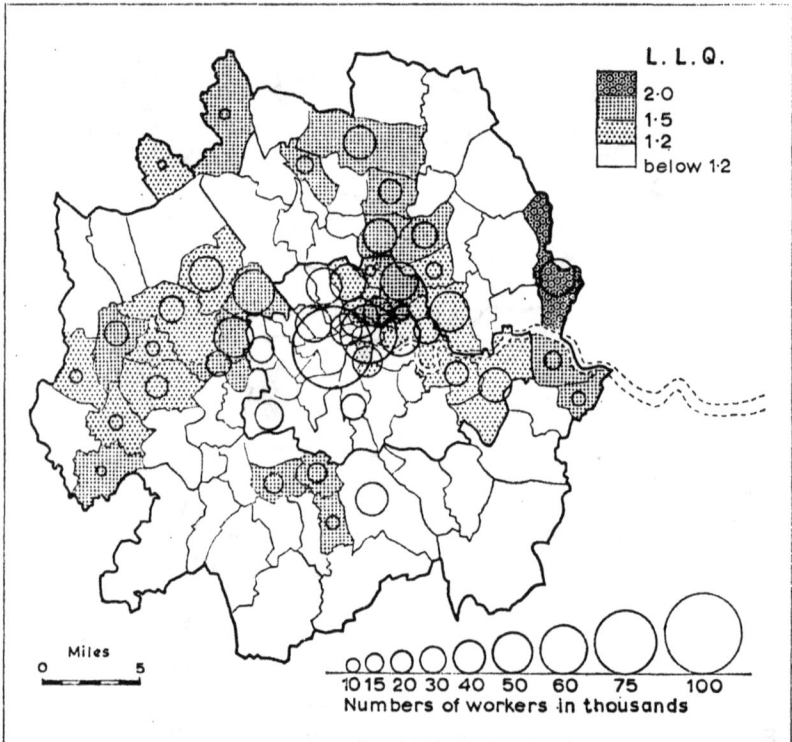

Fig. 2. Greater London: manufacturing industry, 1951 (Source: Census
1951)

The areas thus distinguished on Figure 2 were grouped into five
main areas. First and most important was an enlarged version of
the Victorian manufacturing belt of central, north and east London.
In the centre this now included Holborn. Northwards it had expanded up the west side of the Lea Valley through Hackney,
Tottenham, Edmonton and Enfield; eastwards it had run over the
Lea marshes into West Ham, Leyton and Walthamstow, with an

outlier in Dagenham. This enlarged zone contained in 1951 21 areas with 48 per cent of all the manufacturing workers of Greater London. The second zone of concentration included a large area of western and central Middlesex. It radiated outwards from the borough of Hammersmith, at the western edge of the County of London, westwards to Sunbury at the edge of the Greater London area, north-westwards halfway across Middlesex to Wembley. It thus excluded the areas of far north-west Middlesex (the Harrow-Uxbridge area) and east-central Middlesex (Hendon and Finchley). This zone consisted of 12 areas with 17 per cent of the total workers; six out of the 12 areas had fairly low numbers of manufacturing workers but high L.L.Q.s. In 1861 (so far as can be calculated) this zone had contained less than 3 per cent of the manufacturing workers of London. The third zone of concentration in 1951 was in east Surrey, and was partly associated with the Wandle Valley. It involved five areas with 6 per cent of manufacturing workers. The fourth concentration, a minor one, was along the south bank of the Thames between Greenwich and Erith. This contained four areas and 5 per cent of manufacturing workers. A fifth zone of concentration, in south Hertfordshire at the northern edge of the Greater London area, had three areas containing 1 per cent of all manufacturing workers. It was really a statistical accident arising from the fact of three small areas with exceptional concentrations of manufacturing relative to all workers.

The pattern of manufacturing industry in Greater London may therefore be summarized as follows. During the last hundred years manufacturing in London has been concentrated in a zone radiating from the City and West End towards the northern and eastern boundaries of the present-day County of London. By the mid-twentieth century it had run over these boundaries into east Middlesex and west Essex, on either side of the marshes of the Lea Valley, and had been joined by quite separate smaller concentrations, which were not evident in mid-Victorian London. The most important of these was in western and central Middlesex. This and the smaller areas may be called type cases of the newer sort of industry which developed in London rapidly during the inter-war period, as opposed to the traditional industry of the great Victorian manu-facturing belt.

Most of the rest of this book is devoted to detailed study of the geographical patterns of the major manufacturing industries of London. In this study the concept of two types of manufacturing, the old and the new, carried on to a large extent in separate manufacturing belts, will be found of great value. The older trades of London, which find their home mainly in the Victorian manufacturing belt and its extensions, are discussed in Chapters 4–7. The newer industries, which are best developed in the Middlesex manufacturing belt, are discussed in Chapters 8–12.

The geographical pattern of employment in the service trades is mapped on Figures 3 and 4. These are based on Local Location Quotients alone. This is inevitable because the 1861 statistics refer to place of residence, which even by this date was different from place of work for those services whose workers were largely professional or clerical: finance, administration, professional services. Already in the 30's Dickens had written:

> . . . the early clerk population of Somers and Camden Towns, Islington, and Pentonville, are fast pouring into the City, or directing their steps towards Chancery Lane and the Inns of Court.[6]

While in 1837 the Royal Commission on Municipal Corporations observed:

> It is also to be observed that much of the importance of the City arises from its being the daily resort of great numbers who, as they do not sleep in it, are not strictly a part of its population; and that the prevalence of this habit has been continually on the increase during the present century.[7]

Because it is a relative index, the Local Location Quotient gives a fairer picture of the distribution of service workers in 1861 than would absolute totals, whether for the dormitory suburbs of Victorian London or for the central areas to which workers commuted.

On the basis of L.L.Q.s above unity, Figure 3 shows that in 1861 workers in the service trades were concentrated in a broad crescent round the northern and western peripheries of the present County of London. This stretched from Hackney on the north-eastern corner of the county westwards through Islington, St

Pancras, Hampstead, St Marylebone, Paddington, Kensington, Hammersmith, Fulham (these four last were combined then into one Registration District) and Chelsea. South of the river it extended from Wandsworth through Lambeth and Camberwell to Bermondsey. The main zone of concentration extended on the east into Essex (West Ham) and on the west into Middlesex (Brentford). South of the river most of Surrey was part of the zone of concentration. In the very centre, the Cities of London and Westminster formed another concentration, with 15 per cent of all the service workers of Greater London between them.

Despite the change from a residence to a workplace basis, the 1951 map for services shows that this northern and western zone still persisted, together with the central concentration. Towards the

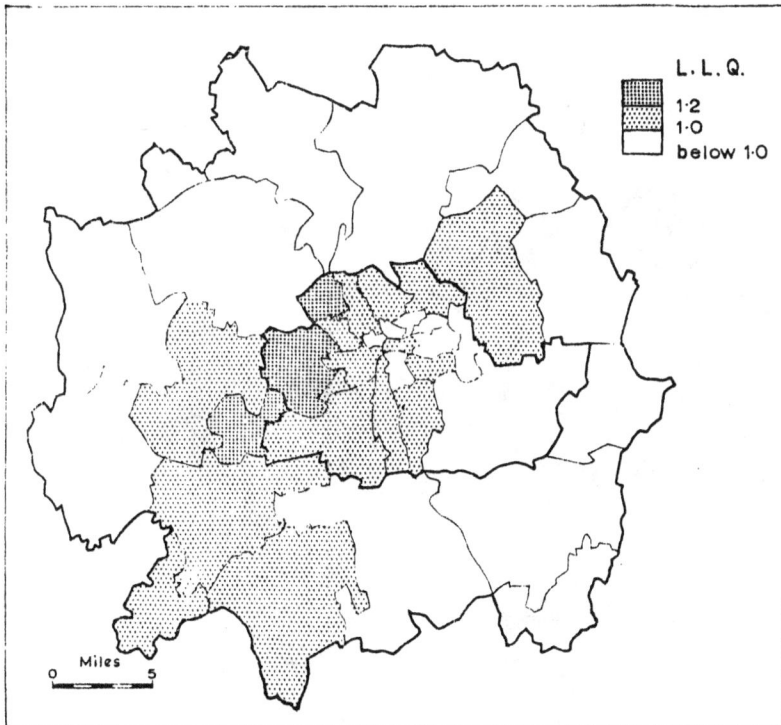

Fig. 3. Greater London: service industry, 1861 (Source: Census 1861. Boundaries in Outer Ring are 1861 Registration Districts)

B

centre, the Cities of London and Westminster, plus the metropolitan
borough of Holborn, accounted for over 25 per cent of the total
employment in services in Greater London. On the edge of the
county, a continuous belt from St Pancras in the east, through the
north-western and western boroughs, and south of the river from
Wandsworth to Lewisham, contained another 25 per cent. (Nearly
4 per cent of this total were, however, in St Marylebone, and many
of these were undoubtedly West End workers.) 64 per cent of the
service workers were in the County of London, as compared with
52 per cent of the manufacturing workers. This reflects the great
pull of the central business district for many of the service trades.

Figure 4 shows that in 1951 the areas of concentration in the
Outer Ring, which were already evident in 1861, had spread widely.
Two main zones may be distinguished. First, a wide belt in central
Middlesex, between the West Middlesex manufacturing belt and the

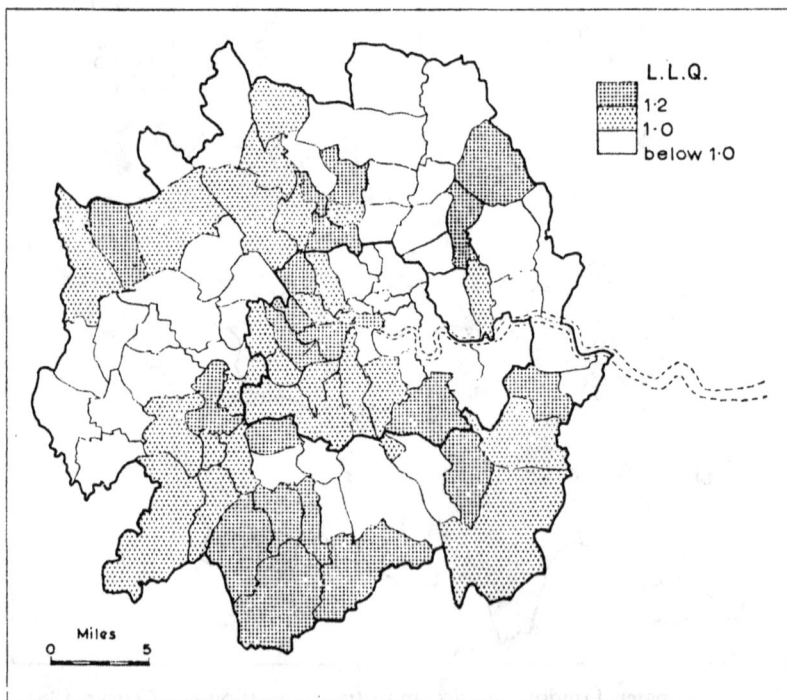

Fig. 4. Greater London: service industry, 1951 (Source: Census 1951)

Lea Valley tongue. It extended from Uxbridge on the north-western corner of the county, through Ruislip, Harrow, Hendon and Finchley, to Southgate and Wood Green in the east. Northwards it spilled out into Barnet. Secondly, the whole of central and western Surrey within the Greater London boundary. These are the residential southern heights of London. They extend from Wimbledon in the north-east to Esher in the south-west. Lastly, there was a smaller concentration in Kent, away from the river, centred on Bexley, Bromley and Orpington.

It must be pointed out, however, that the use of Location Quotients gives these areas a deceptively wide extent. The Middlesex zone contained 11 of the 26 administrative areas of Middlesex, yet it contained only 7 per cent of all service workers of Greater London. Twelve areas in Surrey, out of 16, contained 5 per cent. The five areas in Kent contained 2 per cent. The entire Outer Ring contained only 36 per cent of the total, compared with 23 per cent in the Cities of London and Westminster alone. The reason is simply that these were areas of small total employment, which appeared to contain concentrations of service workers, so to speak, by default. They were the great dormitory areas of London, which exported every weekday a large part of their resident populations into central London. The 11 areas in Middlesex with Quotients for the service trades above unity, for example, suffered a daily net loss of 19·5 per cent of their resident populations to work in other areas during the day in 1951. The 12 Surrey areas suffered a net loss of 16·4 per cent.[8]

This chapter has dealt with a great amount of factual material, and it may be helpful to summarize the main points which have emerged.

1. Today, as in the mid-nineteenth century, London is the greatest single centre of economic activity in the country in terms of numbers employed. In 1951 about one in five of the workers of England and Wales worked in Greater London; in 1861 between one in six and one in seven.

2. Primary industry is not important in London and may be disregarded.

3. Manufacturing industry has tended to concentrate in London to about the same extent as all employment. The ratios given above

for all industry are true at both dates for manufacturing workers too. London has always been the chief centre of manufacturing in the country.

4. Service industry is relatively more important in London than in the whole country. But the degree of concentration in London fell between 1861 and 1951. About a quarter of the country's workers in service trades work in London.

5. Industries may be important in the economy of an area on account of absolute size, or because of relative degree of concentration in the area. In London manufacturing industry, clothing and electrical engineering are examples of the first case; printing, furniture, precision instruments and paint are examples of the second. London has no single staple industry; its biggest industries have Location Quotients close to the national average.

6. Within London, manufacturing and services have concentrated in areas complementary to each other. In 1861 manufacturing was concentrated in the centre, east and north of the County of London area. In 1951 this zone remained but had spread outwards into north Middlesex and Essex, while an important independent zone had developed in West Middlesex. The picture for service industry is more difficult to interpret, but it is certain that the services have been attracted powerfully to central London, drawing their workers from long distances.

1 E. Aves in C. Booth (ed.), *Life and Labour of the People in London* (1892–7), IX, 176.
2 In 1951 12·3 per cent of all workers in the South East Lancashire Conurbation were in cotton textile manufacture. The L.Q. for cotton textile manufacture in the Conurbation was 8·4.
3 H. Jones, *East and West London* (1875), 158–9.
4 Wilfred Smith (ed.), *A Scientific Survey of Merseyside* (British Association, Liverpool 1953), 177.
5 For a general discussion of the competing demands on agricultural land at the present day, see G. P. Wibberley, *Agriculture and Urban Growth* (1960).
6 Charles Dickens, 'The Streets by Morning', *Sketches by Boz* (1836).
7 *Second Report R.C. Municipal Corporations, 3, P.P.* 1837, XXV.
8 *Census 1951, Report on Usual Residence and Workplace* (H.M.S.O. 1956). In 1933 D. H. Smith was able to distinguish clear residential zones in north and north-west Middlesex, separating the manufacturing zones of north-east Middlesex (the Lea Valley) and west Middlesex. D. H. Smith, *The Industries of Greater London* (1933), 10–11.

4

THE OLDER INDUSTRIES: CLOTHING[1]

IN THIS and the next two chapters we shall discuss some of the most important manufacturing industries of the great manufacturing belt of inner London, the belt which dominated the economy of the metropolis in the mid-nineteenth century and has survived and enlarged itself up to the present day. In 1861 this belt, as defined in Chapter 3, contained 55·7 per cent of all the manufacturing workers of London. But it contained 55·4 per cent of the printers, 58·6 per cent of the clothes makers, 64·0 per cent of the workers in the precious metals and precision trades and 72·1 per cent of the furniture makers. Together these groups made up 62·1 per cent of the total manufacturing employment in the manufacturing belt, as compared with 57·7 per cent in Greater London as a whole. In 1951 the enlarged Victorian manufacturing belt contained 48·3 per cent of all the manufacturing workers of London. By then the precision group had largely migrated out of the belt, so that only 43·9 per cent of the London total was found there. But in furniture the Victorian belt had 69·4 per cent of all the workers of Greater London; in printing 73·9 per cent; in clothing 83·8 per cent. Altogether the three groups made up in 1951 44·1 per cent of total employment in manufacturing in the belt, compared with 29·0 per cent in Greater London as a whole. Between 1861 and 1951 the relative degree of concentration of these trades in the belt, as measured by Local Location Quotients, had therefore increased.

As a corollary, these older-established industries tend to be weakly represented in the newer manufacturing areas of London. In 1951 the Middlesex manufacturing zone accounted for 17·3 per cent of all manufacturing workers in Greater London. Its proportion of workers in precision trades was slightly higher, 18·4 per cent. But for furniture the proportion was only 9·1 per cent; for printing 6·0 per cent; and for clothing a mere 2·8 per cent. The four groups

37

together made up only 11·4 per cent of all manufacturing employment in the Middlesex zone, and of this the precision trades
accounted for 4·9 per cent.

Perhaps the most important question that can be asked about
the older industries as a group is: are there, in fact, common factors
in their similar location patterns? If so, how far do they resemble or
differ from the factors affecting the location patterns of the newer
trades to be discussed later in the book? Space can be found to
study only three representative industries: clothing (excluding
footwear), furniture and printing.

Facts of location

The manufacture of clothing (excluding footwear) is the largest
and probably the most representative of the older-established trades.
The Census statistics for the entire clothing industry are set out in
Table 4. They appear to show an industry in slow decline. It is
unlikely, though, that this is real, for clothes have an income
elasticity of demand approximately equal to unity.[2] The explanation
probably lies partly in the fact that makers have been more effec-
tively segregated from dealers in the later Censuses, and partly in
the increasing substitution of capital for labour in the industry.

Two important facts about the location of the industry
emerge.

The first is that clothing is a distinctly metropolitan trade. In
1861 Greater London contained just under one-quarter, and in 1951
just under one-third, of the clothing workers of England and Wales.
Although clothing had lost its predominance by the time of the
1951 Census, it is certain that during the greater part of the last
century it was the most important of the generally recognized major
industrial groups in London in terms of numbers employed.
Excluding those engaged in making and repairing footwear, clothing
workers made up just over 10 per cent of the total labour force of
London in the mid-nineteenth century, and a little under 4 per cent
of a greatly-increased total in the mid-twentieth. In 1861 this percentage was over one and a half times as high, and in 1951 about
one and a half times as high again, as the corresponding percentage
for England and Wales.

TABLE 4

CLOTHING (excluding footwear):

ENGLAND AND WALES, GREATER LONDON, 1861, 1921, 1951

(Source: Censuses, 1861, 1921, 1951)

	1861	*1921*	*1951*
England and Wales			
1 Numbers employed in clothing manufacture, thousands	626·5	586·9	512·0
2 Percentage of clothing to all workers	6·6	3·4	2·6
Greater London			
3 Numbers employed in clothing manufacture, thousands	150·8	180·8	166·5
4 Percentage of clothing to all workers	10·2	5·6	3·9
5 Percentage of London clothing workers to England and Wales clothing workers	24·1	30·8	32·3
6 Location Quotient for clothing in Greater London	1·6	1·6	1·5

The second fact about location is that, at least since the beginning of the period chosen here, clothing manufacture has been localized to a high degree within certain narrowly-defined areas of central and inner suburban London, forming remarkably persistent industrial 'quarters' of the kind described by M. J. Wise for the jewellery and gun trades of Birmingham.[3] Many of the older manufacturing trades established in London before 1914 show similar concentrations, as for instance the furniture quarter of Shoreditch and Bethnal Green, the watchmaking and precision-instruments quarter of Clerkenwell, and the printing quarter of the City and Finsbury. The present extent of these quarters has been delimited in an interesting map by J. E. Martin.[4] The Census and Directory sources, for all their limitations, are found to give a consistent picture of the development and movement of these concentrations over a period. These changes will now be examined in turn for the three branches of the clothing industry most important in London: tailoring; women's dressmaking; and the manufacture of shirts, blouses, overalls and underwear.

TABLE 5

TAILORING: LOCALIZATION WITHIN LONDON, 1861 AND 1951.

(Source: Censuses, 1861 and 1951)

	1861			1951		
	Numbers employed	Percentage of Greater London total	Local Location Quotient	Numbers employed	Percentage of Greater London total	Local Location Quotient
England and Wales	136390	100·0		271055	100·0	
Greater London	36261	95·6		81868	85·7	
County of London	34680	18·5	2·0	70172	12·2	1·1
Westminster M.B.	6724	6·6	1·2	9970	8·2	2·4
St Marylebone M.B.	2397	6·0	0·9	6688	3·9	1·4
St Pancras M.B.	2176	7·7	1·9	3171	4·2	0·5
City	2780	5·6	1·6	3405	1·1	0·5
Holborn M.B.	2021	3·7	0·9	879	6·3	3·3
Finsbury M.B.	1345	17·9	2·3	5160	17·4	7·9
Stepney M.B.	6481	4·3	1·1	14221	4·5	4·0
Shoreditch M.B.	1574	3·5	1·1	3710	2·7	4·7
Bethnal Green M.B.	1276	1·1	0·5	2207	12·6	7·0
Hackney M.B. } Stoke Newington M.B.	410			{ 10280 879	1·1	3·5

	1861	1951
Greater London percentage of England and Wales:	26·6	30·2
Greater London Location Quotient:	1·7	1·4
Greater London Coefficient of Local Concentration:	0·27	0·48

M.B.—Metropolitan Borough

Tailoring. The Census statistics are set out in Table 5. They show two persistent centres of concentration, a West End centre in Westminster and an East End centre which in 1861 was virtually confined to Stepney, but which by 1951 had developed an important outlier in Hackney. Together Westminster and Stepney contained in 1861 nearly 40 per cent of the tailoring workers of Greater London; in 1951, together with Hackney, almost exactly 40 per cent. The areas of concentration are shown in the key maps for Westminster and Stepney. The Directory entries for the Westminster concentration are plotted in Figures 5 and 6, and those for the Stepney concentration in Figures 7 to 9. These maps show that the central concentrations occupied only small parts of the boroughs concerned, extending for but a few blocks in any direction. The Westminster concentration was limited by Bond Street, Oxford Street, Regent Street and Piccadilly, with an extension east of Regent Street into Soho. It was based on the streets famous in the highest-class men's tailoring: Savile Row, Sackville Street, Maddox Street and Conduit Street. The concentration in Stepney was at the

Fig. 5. Tailoring: West End, 1861 (Source: Directories. No undertakings mapped west of Edgware Road or north of Marylebone Road)

Fig. 6. Tailoring: West End, 1951 (Source: Directories. No undertakings mapped west of Edgware Road or north of Marylebone Road)

extreme western edge of the borough, in Whitechapel, extending westwards into the City of London along Houndsditch and eastwards along the Whitechapel and Commercial Roads only to the New Road or a little beyond; it was limited sharply on the north side by the railway running west–east from Liverpool Street to Bethnal Green, and to the south by Cable Street, marking the northern boundary of Dockland. Figure 10 shows that in 1951 the Hackney concentration spread widely through the southern half of the borough.

Women's outerwear (*dresses and gowns*). The Census statistics are set out in Table 6. As with tailoring, there are striking West End and East End concentrations; but in detail there are important differences. In the West End concentration the centre of gravity has developed to the north of that in tailoring, so that today the trade is shared almost equally between the modern metropolitan boroughs of Westminster and St Marylebone, lying respectively south and north of Oxford Street. Over the 90-year period, 1861–1951, St Marylebone has gained, relatively, at the expense of the

42

area to the south, although in absolute terms both areas have increased, accounting together for about 20 per cent of all workers in this branch of the industry in Greater London in 1861, and about 30 per cent in 1951. The Directory entries, plotted in Figures 11 and 12, again show the constricted nature of the quarter. The West-

Fig. 7. Tailoring: Stepney and Bethnal Green, 1861 (Source: Directories)

minster section, which contains more firms using the old style of 'dressmaker', has concentrated especially round the north end of New Bond Street and along South Molton Street. The St Marylebone section, relatively unimportant in 1861, was concentrated by 1951 in the streets immediately north and east of Oxford Circus,

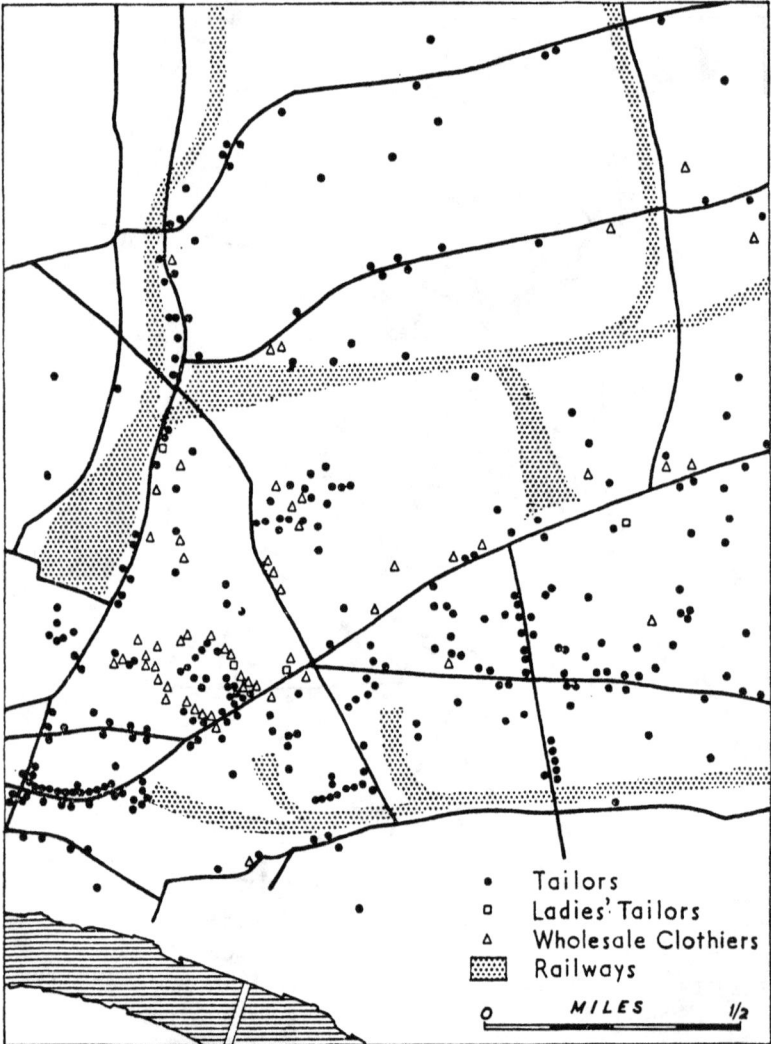

Fig. 8. Tailoring: Stepney and Bethnal Green, 1901 (Source: Directories)

bounded approximately by Regent Street (above Oxford Circus), Mortimer Street, Newman Street and Oxford Street; here, in 1951, most of the firms describing themselves as 'gown makers' were found. The East End centre was less important, relatively, than in tailoring; it was also in 1951 more closely restricted to the borough

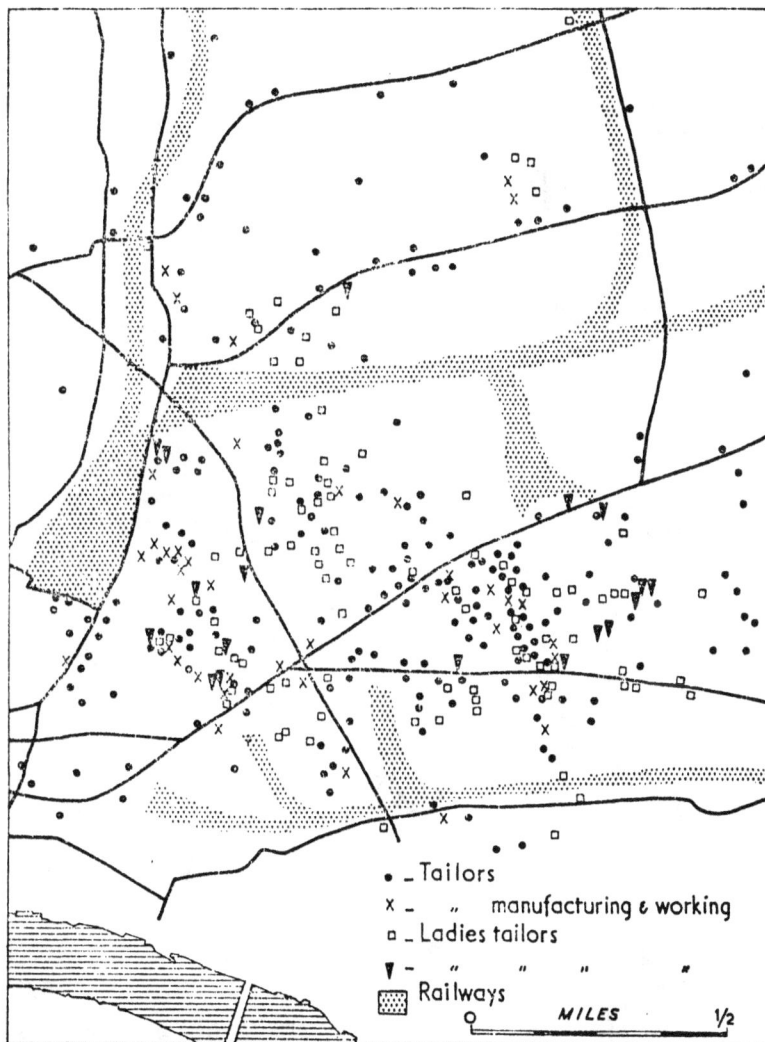

Fig. 9. Tailoring: Stepney and Bethnal Green, 1951 (Source: Directories)

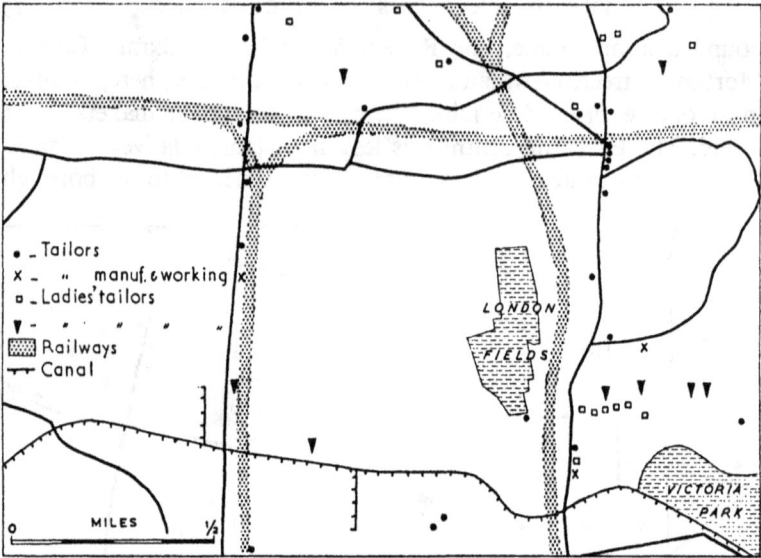

Fig. 10. Tailoring: Hackney, 1951 (Source: Directories)

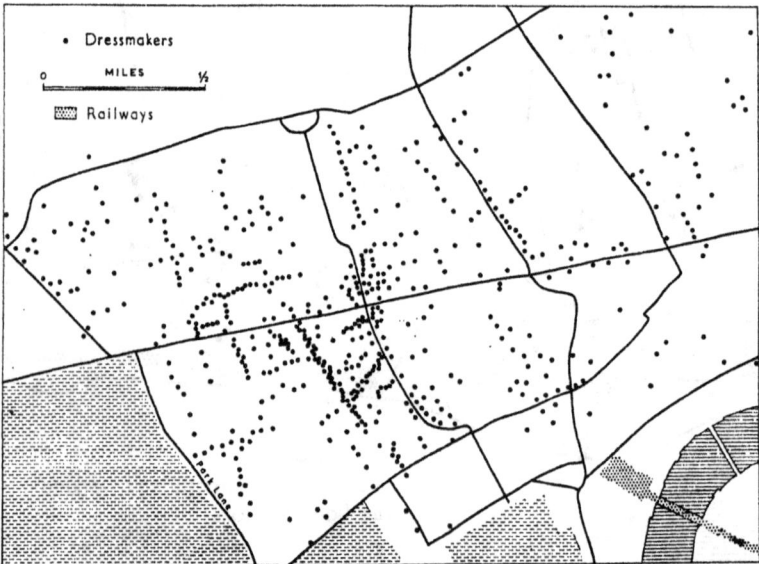

Fig. 11. Women's outerwear: West End, 1861 (Source: Directories. No undertakings mapped west of Edgware Road or north of Marylebone Road)

TABLE 6

WOMEN'S OUTERWEAR: LOCALIZATION WITHIN LONDON, 1861 AND 1951

(Source: Censuses, 1861 and 1951)

	1861			1951		
	Numbers employed	Percentage of Greater London total	Local Location Quotient	Numbers employed	Percentage of Greater London total	Local Location Quotient
England and Wales	286298			114827		
Greater London	59894	100·0		54663	100·0	
County of London	54880	91·6		43501	79·6	
Westminster M.B.	6173	10·3	1·1	7798	14·3	1·3
St Marylebone M.B.	5308	8·9	1·6	9126	16·7	4·9
St Pancras M.B.	4931	8·2	1·3	2526	4·6	1·6
City	2081	3·5	0·9	1792	3·3	0·4
Holborn M.B.	1939	3·2	0·9	246	0·4	0·2
Finsbury M.B.	2699	4·5	1·2	2173	4·0	2·1
Stepney M.B.	4279	7·1	0·9	6752	12·3	5·6
Shoreditch M.B.	3240	5·4	1·4	1146	2·1	1·9
Bethnal Green M.B.	1401	2·3	0·8	510	0·9	1·6
Hackney M.B.	} 1302	2·2	0·9	{ 3207	5·9	3·3
Stoke Newington M.B.				682	1·3	4·0

	1861	1951
Greater London percentage of England and Wales:	20·9	47·6
Greater London Location Quotient:	1·3	2·2
Greater London Coefficient of Local Concentration:	0·10	0·41

M.B.—Metropolitan Borough

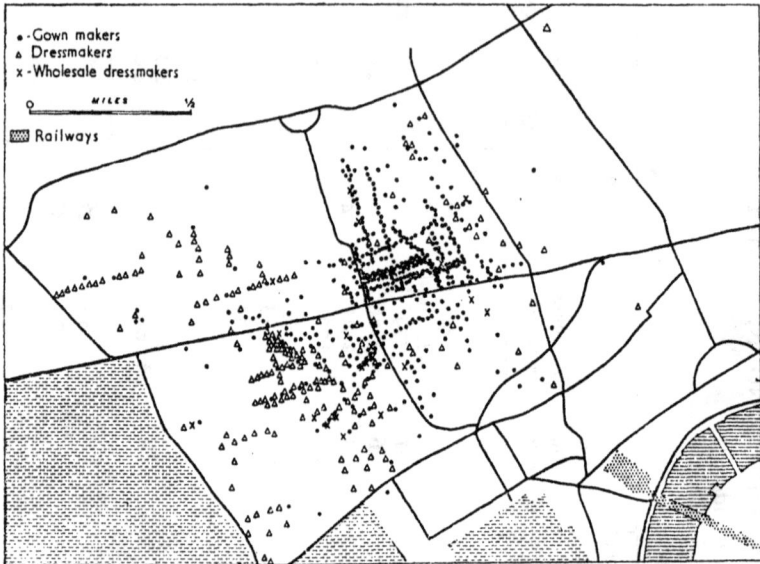

Fig. 12. Women's outerwear: West End, 1951 (Source: Directories. No undertakings mapped west of Edgware Road or north of Marylebone Road)

of Stepney. The directory entries, plotted in Figures 13 and 14, show that, like the tailors, the Stepney dressmakers were concentrated in Whitechapel, especially along Middlesex Street and the streets which give off it, and along Commercial Road as far as the New Road corner.

Shirts, blouses, overalls and underwear. The Census statistics are set out in Table 7. Here the degree of concentration has been substantially lower, and has tended to weaken since 1861, so that by 1951 only 65 per cent of the workers in Greater London worked within the London County Council area, compared with 80 per cent in dressmaking and 86 per cent in tailoring. Within this inner area limited concentrations of workers have persisted from 1861 to 1951: one in Westminster, representing Mayfair and Soho, and another in the East End, which spread out between 1861 and 1951 from Stepney into Hackney and Stoke Newington. But these are not 'quarters' on the scale of those in tailoring or dressmaking.

48

TABLE 7
SHIRTS, BLOUSES, OVERALLS AND UNDERWEAR: LOCALIZATION WITHIN LONDON, 1861 AND 1951
(Source: Censuses, 1861 and 1951)

	1861			1951		
	Numbers employed	Percentage of Greater London total	Local Location Quotient	Numbers employed	Percentage of Greater London total	Local Location Quotient
England and Wales	76015			60446		
Greater London	25467	100·0		13997	100·0	
County of London	23935	94·0		9053	64·7	
Westminster M.B.	2771	10·9	1·2	1178	8·4	0·8
St Marylebone M.B.	1723	6·8	1·2	555	4·0	1·2
St Pancras M.B.	1821	7·2	1·1	328	2·3	0·8
City	1122	4·4	1·1	681	4·9	0·6
Holborn M.B.	1114	4·4	1·3	82	0·6	0·2
Finsbury M.B.	1250	4·9	1·3	726	5·2	2·7
Stepney M.B.	4628	18·2	2·3	597	4·3	1·9
Shoreditch M.B.	1546	6·1	1·6	629	4·5	4·0
Bethnal Green M.B.	904	3·6	1·1	82	0·6	1·0
Hackney M.B.	600	2·4	1·0	954	6·8	3·8
Stoke Newington M.B.				440	3·1	10·1

	1861	1951
Greater London percentage of England and Wales:	33·5	23·2
Greater London Location Quotient:	2·1	1·1
Greater London Coefficient of Local Concentration:	0·26	0·40

M.B.—Metropolitan Borough

Factors in location

Two main features of the location of the clothing industry call for explanation: first, its markedly metropolitan character; second, the concentration of the tailoring and dressmaking branches in industrial quarters within inner London. The factors which might be

Fig. 13. Women's outerwear: East End, 1861 (Source: Directories)

thought to influence the location of the industry are examined in turn.

Materials. These are unimportant, for two reasons. First, the materials are textiles, that is, semi-manufactures, and relatively light; compared with most industries, their cost represents a rela-

Fig. 14. Women's outerwear: East End, 1951 (Source: Directories)

tively small part of total production costs. This should postulate a
fairly footloose pattern of location,[5] which is not the case. Secondly,
in Britain the cloth invariably travels to the place of manufacture
carriage-paid, so that its transport cost to the clothing manufacturer
is nil, and no location can on this ground enjoy a cost advantage
over another.[6]

Fuel and power. Neither are these important. As Factory
Inspector Henderson put it in his report on industry in London
in 1877:

> . . . the most important of these labour-saving machines, so
> far as the metropolis is concerned, is the sewing machine. By
> the aid of this most ingenious and useful instrument it has
> become practicable to make of the dense population of London
> a great manufacturing community. Situated as it is at a great
> distance from any of our important coalfields the high price of
> fuel is an effectual barrier to the use of steam as a motive power,
> and the surplus labour of London could never be utilised with
> profit in any branch of manufacture where such a power was
> necessary on a large scale. But the sewing machine gives all the
> advantages derived from a labour-saving machine without the
> intervention of mechanical power, and hence the rapidity and
> universality of its adoption in London.[7]

Market. In the clothing trades the finished product, like the raw
material, is so valuable (relative to bulk and weight) that variations
in the cost of getting it to market among different firms in this
country are always less than 1 per cent of total costs.[8] The real
importance of the market for the industry is not susceptible to
measurement in any ordinary cost terms; yet it is critical. It lies in
the basic fact of most clothing manufacture: that, because of the
importance of individual fit and the capricious and unpredictable
trends of style, close and frequent contact with the market is im-
perative. But during the last hundred years great changes have
occurred in the way clothes are made and sold in the different
branches of the trade, and because of these the market has meant
different things at different times for these different branches, with
important effects on location.

1. *The retail bespoke system.* The simplest case is that of men's

retail bespoke tailoring, where a suit is individually cut and made to a particular customer's order and to his measurements, generally by one or at most two craftsmen, without outside help. This system created and for long dominated the West End tailoring quarter. Here a concentration of rich customers, which had segregated itself geographically from Tudor times onwards,[9] came to be waited upon by a concentration of producers, who, because they produced to individual order, had to work close to their market.[10] The older section of the women's dressmaking trade in the West End, the bespoke 'Court dressmakers' west of Regent Street and north of the tailoring quarter, had the same origin; and so indeed did the old bespoke shoe and saddlery trades, among others. Until 1850, and later, middle-class women also got their dresses made on the bespoke system, to humbler styles and in humbler materials, by an army of small suburban dressmakers, who listed themselves in the Post Office Directories. For this reason the women's dressmaking trade in London was much less concentrated in 1850 than it later became.

2. *The wholesale ready-made system.* The retail bespoke method of production is inevitably an expensive one, catering for the limited section of the population that can afford to pay its prices. For the rest of the people, until about 1850:

> Worn clothes were of course always procurable in the purlieus of Whitechapel and St Giles's. A nobleman's or wealthy commoner's cast-off garments went to his domestics, and from the domestics to the old clothesmen, and from the old clothesmen to mechanics, and from the mechanics to the sweepers at the street-crossings. In fact, the poor of all classes were glad to wear at second hand the costumes of the rich, for clothes *made to order* were most disproportionately costly.[11]

But after 1850, the better to meet this demand, there arose, in Beatrice Webb's words:

> . . . a new province of production, inhabited by a peculiar people, working under a new system, with new instruments, and yet separated by a narrow and constantly shifting boundary from the sphere of employment of an old-established native industry.[12]

This 'new province' consisted of the manufacture of cheap new clothes.

> We . . . brought about a wholesome and important revolution in our trade, when we originated the NEW, YET READY-MADE CLOTHING SYSTEM. . . . We filled large store-rooms with cheap and new Ready-made clothes, quite as well finished as those made to order at the most fashionable houses in the town. Our prices, both in the Ready-made and Bespoke Departments of our Establishments, were so low as to excite universal astonishment. . . . Now eighty per cent of the population purchase Ready-made clothing, because the prejudice against it has been conquered by the reputation of our firm.[13]

The claim was made by Messrs Moses, of Aldgate, who were already selling ready-made clothing by 1846.[14] Moses's clothes were perhaps as good as they claimed; but the majority of the clothes produced by the new system were certainly 'cheap clothes and nasty'.[15]

Demand was not the only factor in the arrival of the new system; it needed also a change on the supply side, a technical revolution in the way clothes were made. This industrial revolution came between 1840 and 1890, and has had scant attention from economic historians. It depended on two inventions: the sewing machine, perfected in its modern form by Elias Howe in the United States in 1846; and the band-saw, for cutting many thicknesses of cloth simultaneously, probably invented by John Barran, a wholesale clothier of Leeds, in 1858.[16] From 1850 mass sewing and mass cutting revolutionized the industry technically and economically, but they meant little change in the existing small-scale organization. For the revolution in clothing differed from that in the textile trades in the amount of capital needed. In textiles the machinery was expensive in itself; it needed also a steam-engine to drive it, and a large factory to house it. In clothing, the only piece of machinery costing much money was the band-saw; it also needed some skill in operation. Logically, then, a wholesale clothier did the cutting at his warehouse, and gave out the pieces to be finished on the system of subcontracting, or sweating. In Beatrice Webb's words, 'with £1 in his pocket any man may rise to the dignity of a sweater':

His living-room becomes his workshop, his landlord or his butcher the security; round the corner he finds a brother Israelite whose trade is to supply pattern garments to take as samples of work to the wholesale house; with a small deposit he secures on the hire system both sewing machine and presser's table.[17]

In clothing, then, the Industrial Revolution failed to engender a factory system; on the contrary, it led in the second half of the nineteenth century to a more and more vertically-disintegrated system of production, in which a sweater might subcontract the specialized jobs of pleating, buttonholing, button-covering and embroidering to firms in his area. This system has survived and flourished in this century in the face of competition from provincial factory production, notably in the wholesale bespoke system of men's tailoring evolved shortly after 1900 by Montague Burton in Leeds.[18]

The system of subcontract or sweating might be applied to retail bespoke work. By 1890 the structure of the traditional West End trade was already much affected by the new techniques. The older and more conservative hand tailors, organized as the Amalgamated Society of Tailors, were struggling against the Association of Master Tailors, who were trying to introduce the division-of-labour principle by the substitution of time- for piece-rates.[19] There was already in 1890 a clear division between the best tailors west of Regent Street and the growing army of contractors to the east of it. But in origin the sweating system was associated with the rise of the whole-sale ready-made branch of the industry, in which clothes were made in stock sizes for a wholesale clothier who ordered them in speculation of a profit. This system seems to have arisen first, during the 1840's and 50's, in the East End tailoring trade, which the Census figures reveal to be already important by 1861. The essential factor in the location of this trade was the fact that the market for the goods was not the final consumer, as in bespoke work, but the wholesale house. Up to 1890, ready-made clothing was invariably made for the wholesale house; the manufacturer would supply the draper direct 'in very few instances', because the drapers needed small quantities of such a large number of different articles.[20] But a wholesale dress dealer near St Paul's Churchyard was already complaining in the 80's that

. . . the tendency is for the manufacturer to go more direct to the consumer; and a great many large retail concerns that used to be obliged to get their goods from us, now go direct to the manufacturer; and also the shippers do the same.[21]

This tendency was powerfully reinforced in the twentieth century by the growth of multiple tailoring stores and large department stores; the Census of Production in 1950 showed that in tailoring and dress-making less than 30 per cent of the production went through independent wholesalers.[22] But in the early days the wholesale houses were the origin and end of the productive process, and there is abundant evidence of the hold they had on the location of the sweated trade, through the necessity for frequent personal contact.

Traditionally, these houses were strongly concentrated on the eastern edge of the City of London, and especially in Houndsditch. This was so because they had grown out of the second-hand clothes trade they had replaced, which at least since the sixteenth century was localized in this zone. Already in 1598 Ben Jonson was writing:

Well-bred. Where got'st thou this coat, I mar'le?
Brayne-Worme. Of a *Hounds-ditch* man, sir. One of the deuil's neere kinsmen, a broker.[23]

In Henry Mayhew's account of the mid-nineteenth century, the Jewish old-clothes sellers lived for the most part in the Portsoken ward of Houndsditch.[24] These were the years when old-clothes dealers were fast becoming new-clothes makers; and, of 48 whole-sale clothiers in the Post Office Directory of 1860, 40 were in the City and Whitechapel; 18 in Houndsditch, Minories and adjacent streets alone. Figure 7 shows the distribution of these last in detail. Ninety years later the 1950 Census of Distribution showed that, of the total wholesale trade of Greater London, the City still handled one-third of men's and women's wear.[25]

With these houses constant contact was, and is, necessary, be-cause the vagaries of fashion compel frequent small orders for rapid execution. In the 60's, homework in tailoring might be given out in the afternoon to be finished at noon next day;[26] just after the turn of this century, the wife of an East End dock labourer engaged in homework might spend 8*d.* return three times a week in getting her work to and from the warehouse.[27] The ever-present problems of time and cost involved in contact with the warehouse were alleviated a little in the late nineteenth century by the development of intermediate middlemen between the warehouse and the final contractor, and by the growth of East End branch warehouses; and further in the twentieth century by the coming of the telephone and more rapid urban transport. But still the makers of contracted clothes must locate themselves within narrow geographical limits, circumscribed by the need for frequent and rapid contact. It is this factor that primarily explains the concentrations of both men's tailoring and women's outerwear in Whitechapel.[28] To some extent the Stepney men's trade has altered its character in this century, coming more and more to produce bespoke goods for West End order;[29] but the usual East End bespoke suit is cut to a stock pattern, and its production is combined with that of ready-made clothing.[30]

3. *The retail ready-made system.* The ready-made system of production, then, had invaded both men's tailoring and women's outwear by 1861 and had produced a distinct industrial quarter in Whitechapel. About two decades later it began profoundly to affect the old West End women's outerwear trade. In 1861 the West End dressmaker was still usually a Court dressmaker, producing individual dresses to order for a limited public, with acute seasonal pressures; in such houses work would often continue far into the night before a 'Royal Drawing Room'.[31] But as early as 1881 a guide to industry in London could say of millinery, dressmaking and ladies' underclothing:

> The manufacturers aim at producing a quick-selling, quickly perishable article, so that one not in constant employment falls behind in knowledge of the trade.[32]

In the 90's large shops were already established near Oxford Street.[33] These integrated manufacturing and selling functions; a survey in 1881 had shown that 25 large drapers in the west and west-central districts had 1500 sales assistants and 4000 workroom assistants.[34] By 1902 the Factory Inspector could say:

> For good or for evil, and, I believe, on the whole, decidedly for the good of workers and consumers, the great masses of our

countrywomen (of artizan and manual labouring classes, and of
upper and lower middle classes) are already being largely clad in
'ready-made' dresses and mantles and millinery supplied by
factory organisation.[35]

The army of high-class Court and private dressmakers, the Inspector
thought, would remain in the West End, because there would always
be a demand for their services from the wealthier classes and from
the special and exceptional needs of the middle classes; though much
of the ready-made production was already of a very high quality.
Only four years later the Report speaks of fresh inroads made by
the large ready-made houses in the trades of the Court dressmaker.[36]
The small private dressmaker now often became a contracting outworker for the big workshop; she found regular work there, she lost
no time in fitting customers, she did not have to find her own
materials, and she was paid weekly.[37]

   Thus another 'province of production' was created. But this time
it remained close to the old, especially around and north of Oxford
Circus. For in the 80's and 90's, as already described, the hold of
the wholesaler in the ready-made trade was already weakening; so
that, from the first, the new trade produced direct for retail outlets,
and found it necessary to locate itself in close contact with them. In
the first decade of this century the Tube railways finally confirmed
the primacy of Oxford Street and Regent Street as the first shopping
streets of London. The first line in the West End, the Central
London, was opened under Oxford Street in 1900; in 1907 the
Bakerloo line came under Regent Street and connected with the
Central at Oxford Circus. The Factory Inspectors found in 1907
that the main concentrations of workshops in dressmaking and
ladies' tailoring were around Regent Street and Bond Street; this
they ascribed to the opening of the Tubes.[38]

   By 1910 City and East End firms were opening branch factories
around and north of Oxford Circus in order to be close to their
retail outlet, a measure of the weakening power of the wholesaler.[39]
During the interwar period the volume of wholesale trade in
women's outerwear probably declined relative to total trade because of the growth of ready-made factory clothing sold direct to
retailers, though in absolute terms it probably increased.[40] It is,
of course, the rise of this new retail ready-made trade which explains

the distinction within the West End quarter in 1951 between the older West End trade around Bond Street, where most firms still describe themselves as 'dressmakers', and the newer 'gown makers' north and east of Oxford Circus. But some of the latter firms had by this time found their way to Stepney, for reasons to be explained later.

Labour. The importance of contact with the market explains the location of some parts of the industry close to West End retail outlets, and of other parts close to City wholesale houses. What is still not clear is why the wholesale section should congregate so particularly in Whitechapel rather than any other area close to the City. The explanation for this lies in labour supply. Today in the London clothing trades employers compete for supplies of scarce labour.[41] But at least until the turn of the century many observers thought that London's critical advantage in clothing manufacture consisted in the exploitation of a great pool of cheap unskilled labour. The subcontract system in the provinces, it was pointed out, went unaccompanied by the distress associated with it in London.[42]

The system of labour exploitation which developed in the clothing trades of late-nineteenth-century London rested upon the conjunction of two circumstances: an almost unlimited demand for cheap unskilled labour, and an almost unlimited supply. The demand sprang from the fact that in the manufacture of cheap clothing capital could not economically be substituted, beyond a point that was soon reached, for cheap unskilled labour. As a London tailor put it in the 80's:

> ... our trade, unfortunately being an easy trade to obtain a small knowledge of, is one to which they [*foreign immigrants*] rush in very large numbers.[43]

Or, in the Covent Garden saying of the eighteenth century, 'Cucumbers two a penny, tailors twice as many'.[44] It took only one or two weeks' education to make one part of a garment on the division-of-labour principle, and in this way trousers might be made for $4\frac{1}{2}d.$ a pair.[45] Trousers, vests and juvenile suits in particular needed little style, and were most easily made by cheap labour for a working-class and colonial market.[46]

This demand met in London an almost inexhaustible supply of

labour willing to accept unskilled work at almost any price. Offering cautionary advice to a young man proposing to seek his fortune in London, *Bentley's Miscellany* commented in 1844:

> Let him recollect, in the first place, that the London labour-market is always overstocked.[47]

And nearly 50 years later an observer noticed that in all trades not needing apprenticeship London had an excess of labour, so that a kind of Gresham's Law operated: cheap bad labour drove out better.[48] Skill in the clothing trades was scarce, and well rewarded,[49] but the lowest labour had no minimum. The principal source of this latter sort of labour was the East End, traditional home of the poor since the sixteenth century.[50]

The East End labour pool contained two main elements. In the words of a witness before the Select Committee of the House of Lords on the Sweating System, in the 80's:

> My contention is, you know, that the cause of sweating is the surplus or surfeit of uneducated or unskilled labour. That is the whole origin of the thing; and is caused by the immigration of Jews, and by the Jewish Board of Guardians, and by the large proportion of women who work at the trade. That is what the surplus is composed of.[51]

Chronologically the women came first: in 1861, so far as figures can be accurately established, the three branches of the clothing trades discussed in this chapter contained in Greater London about 22,000 men to more than 98,000 women; while in the East End (Stepney, Bethnal Green, Shoreditch, Hackney, Stoke Newington and Poplar) the ratio was 5200 : 24,300. Even after the great Jewish immigration of the 80's the women seemed to have formed the rock-bottom of the labour market; working at home, they undersold Jewish male labour in workshops.[52] Possibly the worst case of sweating recorded in the minutes of the Sweating Committee was made by a woman outworker for a Gentile sweater; it was a two-piece knickerbocker suit made for 4½*d*.[53] Homework was a system ideally suited to the seasonal nature of much of the London clothing industry, and there was a vast army of women waiting for the chance to undertake it. This army contained various elements: the shabby-genteel, 'the daughters of poor clergymen and Non-conformist ministers, half-pay officers, or tradesmen who had suffered reverses',[54] who lacked all skill save with the needle; skilled dressmakers from the West End shops, who had lost their skill or their dress sense as they got older, and 'drift away eastward';[55] and, most important, those in reduced circumstances due to old age, illness, widowhood or the unemployment of the husband. It was this last group that was so heavily concentrated in the East End. Over half of the clothes-making homeworkers investigated in West Ham in 1907 were the wives of builders, general labourers and dock labourers, who suffered from irregular employment.[56] Figures to show the exact distribution of the homeworkers are not available until the Factory and Workshop Act of 1901 required employers of outworkers to submit regular lists to the local authorities. In 1907, a typical year, the returns showed that more than four-fifths of all recorded outworkers in the country were clothing workers; that over one-third of the country's outworkers in clothing were in the County of London alone; and that of these more than one-third took their work from firms in the City and the East End boroughs.[57] Such workers must live close to their source of livelihood. But, equally, the firms found it most advantageous to locate themselves near to the largest pools of labour.

The other element in the labour pool was provided by the Jewish immigrants. The Jewish colony in London dates from 1655, when Cromwell lifted the medieval ban on Jewish residence in England. In the eighteenth century political disturbances in Europe brought successive new arrivals. They tended to settle in London beyond the City limits, especially to the east, where they established their own industries in order to avoid apprenticeship to a Christian master. Until 1832 Jews could not become City freemen, and so could not open shops within the City. By the mid-eighteenth century they had established themselves in clothes dealing at the edge of the City, turning in the mid-nineteenth century to the manufacture of ready-made clothes.[58] By 1881 nearly 20 per cent of the population of parts of Whitechapel was foreign-born. But the great wave of immigration followed in the years 1881–6, arising from persecution in Russia and Poland.[59] In these years between 20,000 and 30,000 East

European Jews entered London, and most went to Whitechapel. By 1889 East London was estimated to contain 60,000 to 70,000 Jews, rather less than half of them foreign-born;[60] in 1891 82 per cent of the Russian- and Polish-born inhabitants of London were enumerated in Whitechapel, St George's in the East and Mile End Old Town, covering a total area of about two square miles.[61] Of all immigrants into this country without through tickets in the years 1891–3, inclusive, London was the destination of three-quarters; and this included a high proportion of the destitute, since those with money used it for a through passage to America via Hull and Liverpool.[62] Another peak of immigration began in 1906; and even in 1930, when the second generation of Jewish population had become rather more mobile, the *New Survey of London Life and Labour* estimated that more than half the Jews of East London were still in Stepney, whose population was 43 per cent Jewish.[63] It appears that at that time nearly 30 per cent of the Jewish population of Greater London was still in Stepney and 56 per cent in inner East London, including Hackney and Stoke Newington.[64] After 1945 Lipman doubts whether there were more than 30,000 Jews left in inner East London, out of some 280,000 in Greater London.[65]

For this concentration there were good reasons. East London was the traditional home of the Jews before 1880; it was also the area adjacent to the docks where the immigrants landed. In many cases the new arrivals knew no English; often their only English words were 'Board of Guardians';[66] the only jobs open to them were run by their compatriots in the East End; the institutions that helped them—the Board of Guardians, the Jews' Shelter, the Soup Kitchen, the free schools, the synagogues—were all here; and outside this limited area prejudice was a factor to contend with.[67] As the wretched position of the immigrants improved, these factors became less powerful; but the force of inertia remained.

There were equally good reasons why the Jewish immigrants should crowd into the clothing trades. The ready-made section of the industry, like the area, was traditionally East European Jewish before the great wave of immigration began. The first arrivals therefore went into it; and, later, friends and relations naturally joined them.[68] There were great difficulties for the immigrant who wanted to enter a different industry: even if he had been apprenticed to another trade in his old country he was not accustomed to British methods, he could not as an adult be re-apprenticed here, while the observance of the Sabbath caused difficulties in working alongside Christians. But there were also positive advantages in the clothing trades. Here it was relatively easy for the immigrant to set up as a small master, which he preferred; here was an acutely seasonal trade to which his elastic living standards were suited.[69] Here indeed was an apprenticeship system, of a sort:

> Then perhaps you will describe to us how you learnt your trade?
> I had a nice suit of clothes, though I had no money; I pledged that suit and obtained half-a-sovereign, and I gave that half-a-sovereign to the sweater who taught me the machine work. I had very little to eat, half-a-quartern loaf and a herring for my meals during the time I was apprenticed to the sweater.
> How long was that?
> Four weeks for nothing, besides the half-a-sovereign; and after the four weeks he gave me 6s. a week.[70]

And a labour exchange:

> There is a slave market, a certain place, or rather two places, one on Saturday and one on Sunday, in the East End of London ... One at the other end of Golston-street, and the other would be in Whitechapel, the corner of Commercial-street; they parade there, walk up and down, or talk to each other, and wait until the sweater comes for them.[71]

The Jews were said in 1888 to have created the cheap clothing trade within the last 40 years.[72] The method consisted not in sweating skilled labour—that would have been impossible—but in substituting unskilled for skilled labour wherever possible;[73] and this unskilled labour, completely 'green', hardly even knowing the language, was phenomenally exploitable. Its living standard was minimal; a halfpenny loaf plus some fish refuse might constitute its day's meal;[74] and it was in no position to bargain. The industry based on this labour pool was locked, in Beatrice Webb's classic description for Charles Booth's survey of London life and labour in the late 80's, in a narrow area only one square mile in extent, an area completely divorced economically, socially and culturally from the English population that surrounded it on all sides. The Jewish industry of Whitechapel in those years was related to English industry in the same way as colonial industry was: it competed with the mechanical superiority of late Victorian England in a trade where this superiority counted for relatively little, by using enormous amounts of labour at minimum cost. These lowest levels of the London clothing industry, in which goods of minimum standard were produced by people living at a minimum standard, were bound to disappear with increasing employment possibilities for women, the restriction in 1911 of further alien immigration, workshop legislation, increased factory competition, and the steadily more exacting demands of the market.[75] By the time of the New Survey in 1930 the East London colony had matured industrially. But it tended to remain where it was, with some diffusion northward and eastward.

External economies. In this century the London clothing trades have in fact been remarkably sluggish in responding as the forces of concentration have weakened; not merely the changes in the labour market, but also technical changes such as the increased use of the telephone should, it might be thought, have done more than they have to free the industry from the traditional quarters. This inertia may largely be explained by references to what A. Marshall called specific external economies, which apply to the clothing industry with especial force:

> When an industry has thus chosen a locality for itself, it is likely to stay there long: so great are the advantages which people following the same skilled trade get from near neighbourhood to one another. The mysteries of the trade become no mysteries; but are as it were in the air, and children learn many of them unconsciously. Good work is rightly appreciated, inventions and improvements in machinery, in processes and the general organization of the business have their merits promptly discussed: if one man starts a new idea, it is taken up by others and combined with suggestions of their own; and thus it be-

THE OLDER INDUSTRIES: CLOTHING

comes the source of further new ideas. And presently subsidiary trades grow up in the neighbourhood, supplying it with implements and materials, organizing its traffic, and in many ways conducing to the economy of its material.[76]

In few other trades do so many people start new ideas as in clothing; and in few trades is the importance of subsidiary trades so keenly felt, because few other trades are quite so disintegrated into separate specialist processes. Thus in Stepney today, despite a trend towards vertically integrated production in large factories, it is still fairly common for a making-up firm to subcontract buttonholing, pleating, embroidering and button-covering to specialist firms;[77] and even if it does not, it must depend on ancillary firms for its supplies of materials—textiles of all sorts, buttons, zips, hooks, belts, decorations, thread, lining materials and the supply and servicing of sewing machines. Such ancillary trades are commonly found in the West End in the side streets on both sides of Oxford Street, southward along Berwick Street into Soho, northward into the Cleveland Street area of St Marylebone; and in the East End in great numbers along Whitechapel High Street. Commonly they style themselves 'Suppliers to the Trade'. In these streets the nature of the 'trade' goes without saying. Among the small furniture shops of the Hackney Road the same sign is seen, but with a different, though equally understood, meaning.

Because of the continued strength of this form of organization, the average clothing firm remains small. The incomplete return in the 1851 Census gave the average tailoring firm in England and Wales 3·2 workers including one-man firms. After a century of advance in the techniques of factory production, the average in 1951 for the tailoring and dressmaking group of the Census of Production was only 32·8 (including working proprietors).[78]

In these circumstances there come into extreme prominence those factors which Alfred Weber described as leading to agglomeration;[79] no small firm may safely remove from the small zone where ideas are created, and where technical services are available. For the big factory, which may create its own new ideas, buy its materials in bulk, and perform all the specialized processes of manufacture itself, a move to the suburbs or even to the provinces might be possible, but even then problematical. For the clothing trades of any

C

commercial metropolis, whether London, Paris, Berlin or Tokyo, Seidman's verdict on the needle trades of New York City holds good:

> Except for men's clothing and cotton garments . . . New York City still dominates the needle trades. Here is the style center. . . . Here are the largest aggregation of workers, the most readily available stocks of raw material, the necessary accessory trades, and the largest and best selling facilities. Here the market is most sensitive, and here begin trends affecting the entire industry.[80]

1 This chapter is largely based on the author's paper, 'The Location of the Clothing Trades in London, 1861–1951', *Institute of British Geographers, Transactions and Papers*, 26 (1960), 155–78.

2 See Colin Clark, *The Conditions of Economic Progress* (1957), 464–8; R. G. D. Allen, 'Expenditure Patterns of Families of Different Types', in O. Lange, F. McIntyre, T. O. Yntema (ed.), *Studies in Mathematical Economics and Econometrics* (Chicago 1942), 196–7; R. Stone, *The Role of Measurement in Economics* (Cambridge 1951), table 4. This last, based on U.S. experience, puts the figure as low as 0·67.

3 M. J. Wise, 'On the evolution of the Jewellery and Gun quarters in Birmingham', *Institute of British Geographers, Transactions and Papers*, 15 (1951), 57–72.

4 J. E. Martin, 'Industry in Inner London', *Town and Country Planning*, 25 (1957), 125–8.

5 Wilfred Smith, 'Mobility in the location of industry in Great Britain', *The Advancement of Science*, 6 (1949–50), 115.

6 D. C. Hague and P. K. Newman, *Costs in Alternative Locations: the Clothing Industry* (National Institute of Economic and Social Research, Occasional Papers, 15, Cambridge 1952), 37.

7 *Reports of the Inspectors of Factories for the half-year ending 30th April, 1877*, 23, *P.P.* 1877, XXIII.

8 Hague and Newman, op. cit., 36–7. But Florence thought it an important item in small tailoring shops because of the two-way transport for a fitting: P. Sargant Florence, *Investment, Location, and Size of Plant* (National Institute of Economic and Social Research: Economic and Social Studies, 7, Cambridge 1948), 46.

9 See F. J. Fisher, 'The Development of London as a centre of conspicuous consumption in the Sixteenth and Seventeenth Centuries', *Transactions of the Royal Historical Society*, 4th series, 30 (1948),

37–50; and M. Dorothy George, *London Life in the XVIIIth Century* (1925), 63.

10 There were already shopkeeping master tailors, selling bespoke garments at retail and employing working tailors, by the early seventeenth century. P. K. Newman, 'The Early London Clothing Trades', *Oxford Economic Papers*, 4 (1952), 244.

11 Elias Moses and Son, *The Growth of an Important Branch of British Industry* (1860), 4.

12 Beatrice Potter in C. Booth (ed.), *Life and Labour of the People in London* (1892–7), IV, 37.

13 Elias Moses, op. cit., 5–6.

14 Elias Moses and Son, *The Past, the Present, and the Future. A public address on the opening of the New Establishment of E. Moses and Son, 154, 155, 156, and 157, Minories, and 83, 84, 85, and 86, Aldgate* (1846), 10.

15 Parson Lot (i.e. Charles Kingsley), *Cheap clothes and Nasty*. Published as preface to *Alton Locke* (Library edition, 1900).

16 For the history of the development of these inventions see *Board of Trade: Working Party Report: Light Clothing* (H.M.S.O. 1947), 8–9; and S. J. Sewell, *A Revolution in the Sewing Machine: The Birth and Development of the Sewing Machine* (1892), *passim*. For the band-saw see also Joan Thomas, *A History of the Leeds Clothing Industry*, (Yorkshire Bulletin of Economic and Social Research, Occasional Paper, no. 1, 1955), 9–10.

17 Beatrice Potter, op. cit., 60.

18 Joan Thomas, op. cit., chap. 5 *passim*. Essentially the wholesale bespoke system is a cross between the retail bespoke and the whole-sale ready-made. The customer's individual measurements are invariably referred to one of a large number of patterns, to which the suit is cut. The making-up is done by machinery on the division-of-labour principle.

19 *R. C. Labour, Minutes, Group C*, Q. 14155, 14602–3, *P.P.* 1892, XXXVI, part II.

20 *R. C. Depression of Trade and Industry, Second Report, Minutes*, Q. 3985–6, *P.P.* 1886, XXI.

21 Ibid., Q. 4070.

22 *Census of Production 1950*, vol. 7 (H.M.S.O. 1953).

23 Ben Jonson, *Every Man in his Humour*, folio of 1616, iii, v.

24 Henry Mayhew, *London Labour and the London Poor* (edition of 1861), II, 121.

25 *Census of Distribution 1950*, vol. 3, *Wholesale trade* (H.M.S.O. 1955).

26 Dr. E. Smith, *Sanitary circumstances of tailors in London*. Appendix to *Sixth Report of the Medical Officer of the Privy Council, 425, P.P.* 1864, XXVIII.

27 *S. C. Home Work, Minutes*, 1908, Q. 1821–2, *P.P.* 1908, VIII.

28 In the 80's a sweater could say that a sweatshop must be in a district

close to the City, such as Whitechapel or Spitalfields. *S. C. Sweating System, Minutes*, Q. 8650, *P.P.* 1888, XX.

29 D. L. Munby, *Industry and Planning in Stepney* (Oxford 1951), 191.

30 *New Survey of London Life and Labour* (1930–5), II, 266–9.

31 Dr W. Ord, *Sanitary Circumstances of Dressmakers and Other Needlewomen in London*. Appendix to *Sixth Report of the Medical Officer of the Privy Council*, 364–5, *P.P.* 1864, XXVIII.

32 H. L. Williams, *The Worker's Industrial Index to London* (1881), 22.

33 Frances Hicks in F. W. Galton (ed.), *Workers on their industries* (1895), 16.

34 *Annual Report of the Chief Inspector of Factories*, 1881, 33, *P.P.* 1882, XVIII. The workrooms attached to department stores probably began by making bespoke garments, but started ready-made production in order to keep their staffs busy in slack seasons. M. Wray, *The Women's Outerwear Industry* (1957), 18, 34–5.

35 *Annual Report of the Chief Inspector of Factories*, 1902, 148, *P.P.* 1903, XII.

36 Ibid., 1906, 189, *P.P.* 1907, X.

37 Ibid., 1909, 124, *P.P.* 1910, XXVIII.

38 Ibid., 1907, 148, *P.P.* 1908, XII.

39 Ibid., 1910, 112, *P.P.* 1911, XXII.

40 M. Wray, op. cit., 34.

41 See Hague and Newman, op. cit., 58. But the industry still apparently looks for cheap immigrant labour when it can: in August 1958 an advertisement for machinists appeared in English and Greek in the area of recent Cypriot immigration west of Tottenham Court Road.

42 *S. C. Sweating System, Appendix O:* Report from the Labour Correspondent of the Board of Trade on the Sweating System in Leeds, 605, *P.P.* 1889, XIV, part I.

43 R. C. Labour, Minutes, Group C, op. cit., Q. 14693.

44 M. Dorothy George, op. cit., 211.

45 R. C. Labour, Minutes, Group C, op. cit., Q. 14693.

46 Beatrice Potter, op. cit., 62–4.

47 J. Fisher Murray, 'The physiology of London life', *Bentley's Miscellany*, 15 (1844), 627.

48 W. H. Wilkins, *The Alien Invasion* (1892), 76–7.

49 Beatrice Potter, op. cit., 61.

50 M. Dorothy George, op. cit., 64–5.

51 S. C. Sweating System, Minutes, op. cit., Q. 9610.

52 Clara E. Collet in *Board of Trade Report on the Volume and Effects of Recent Immigration from Eastern Europe*, 114, *P.P.* 1894, LXVIII; S. C. Sweating System, Minutes, op. cit., Q. 3267–71; *S. C. Home Work, Minutes, 1907*, Q. 3305–8, *P.P.* 1907, VI.

53 S. C. Sweating System, Minutes, op cit., Q. 1312, 8813.

54 W. F. Neff, *Victorian Working Women* (1929), 116, quoting Lord Ashley.

55 Dr W. Ord, op. cit., 370.
56 E. G. Howarth and M. Wilson, *West Ham: A Study in Social and Industrial Problems* (Report of the Outer London Inquiry Committee, 1907), 268–9.
57 *Report of the Chief Inspector of Factories on the Administration of the Factory and Workshops Act, 1901, by Local Authorities in respect of Workshops, Outwork, etc., 1907, P.P.* 1909, XXI. Comparison with other years is impossible because of deficiencies in the returns.
58 V. D. Lipman, *Social History of the Jews in England, 1850–1950* (1954), 12–13.
59 For the Jews' handicaps in Eastern Europe see G. Halpern, *Die Jüdischen Arbeiter in London* (Stuttgart and Berlin 1903), chapter 1.
60 H. Llewellyn Smith in Booth, op. cit., III, 100–13.
61 Board of Trade Report on Immigration, op. cit., 36. For the distribution c. 1900, see the map in V. D. Lipman, op. cit., 94–5. This is based on an original in C. Russell and H. S. Lewis, *The Jew in London* (1900), xxxii.
62 Board of Trade Report on Immigration, op. cit., 10. Between one-third and one-sixth of the London arrivals were estimated by various witnesses to be absolutely destitute. *Select Committee of the House of Commons on Emigration and Immigration (Foreigners), Minutes, 1889:* Q.680–2, 728–9, *P.P.* 1889, X.
63 New Survey of London Life and Labour, op. cit., VI, 293.
64 Calculated from New Survey, ibid., and H. L. Trachtenberg, 'Estimate of the Jewish Population of London in 1929', *Journal of the Royal. Statistical Society*, 96 (1933), 96.
65 V. D. Lipman, op. cit., 168–9.
66 *S. C. Emigration, Minutes, 1888:* Q.1210, *P.P.* 1888, XI.
67 Board of Trade Report on Immigration, op. cit., 36–9.
68 S. C. Emigration, Minutes, 1888, op. cit., Q. 1201–3.
69 Board of Trade Report on Immigration, op. cit., 39–43.
70 S. C. Sweating System, Minutes, op. cit., Q. 2832–3.
71 Ibid., Q. 3713–14.
72 S. C. Emigration, Minutes, 1888, op. cit., Q. 2220, 3001.
73 Beatrice Potter, op. cit., 53n.
74 S. C. Emigration, Minutes, 1888, op. cit., Q. 1006–9.
75 S. P. Dobbs, *The Clothing Workers of Great Britain* (Studies in Economic and Political Science, 96, 1928), 164–9.
76 A. Marshall, *Principles of Economics* (8th edition, 1920), 271.
77 D. L. Munby, op. cit., 168.
78 *Census of Great Britain, 1851, P.P.* 1852–3, LXXXVIII, part I; and *Census of Production 1951*, vol. 7 (H.M.S.O. 1953).
79 A. Weber, *Über den Standort der Industrien*, Teil I: *Reine Theorie des Standorts* (Tübingen 1909), especially 125–6; and the volumes on particular industries, e.g. Teil II, Heft 4: W. Haenger, *Die Musikinstrumenten-Industrie* (Tübingen 1919), especially on the concentra-

tion of the industry in Berlin arising from the large pool of skilled labour there, which could provide workers for any section of the industry.

80   Joel Seidman, *The Needle Trades* (Labor in Twentieth Century America, New York, 1942), 8.

5

THE OLDER INDUSTRIES: FURNITURE

FURNITURE is a second example of a large old-established East End trade. Its organization and particular location patterns provide an interesting contrast to those of clothing, for there are many similarities but certain differences, especially in the evolution of the industry since 1900.

As with clothing, the facts of location will first be set out; then an attempt will be made to explain the location patterns in terms of the evolving structure of the industry since 1861.

Facts of location

The Census statistics in Table 8 show that the labour force of the furniture industry expanded between 1861 and 1951 at about the same rate as did the total labour force of the country. It may safely be assumed that with increasing mechanization the product of the industry expanded much faster than this. The rate of increase accords with the majority of income and expenditure studies which have shown that furniture has an income elasticity of demand above unity.[1] The industry has been concentrated in London to a high extent and to a remarkably consistent degree; at all three dates, 1861, 1921 and 1951, just under two-fifths of all workers in England and Wales were enumerated there. But the Location Quotient dropped, because over the period London's share of all industry rose.

Table 9, see p. 81, shows that within London the industry has concentrated in the north-east sector and that since the mid-nineteenth century the degree of concentration there has risen. The Victorian manufacturing belt in 1861 contained 72 per cent of the furniture workers of Greater London; in 1951 its enlarged equivalent contained 73 per cent. But these figures conceal a marked shift of location outwards from the inner districts of the north-east sector to the outer. In 1861 there was a considerable West End branch of the trade, in the City of Westminster and the boroughs of St Marylebone and St Pancras, which together contained nearly 28 per cent of the total workers. A central group—Holborn, Finsbury and Southwark—contained another 19 per cent. The biggest branch of the industry was in the inner East End boroughs of Shoreditch, Bethnal Green and Stepney, with 31 per cent of the total. By 1951

TABLE 8

FURNITURE: ENGLAND AND WALES,

GREATER LONDON, 1861, 1921, 1951

(Source: Censuses, 1861, 1921, 1951)

	1861	1921	1951
England and Wales			
1 Numbers employed in furniture manufacture, thousands	66·4	102·2	161·7
2 Percentage of furniture to all workers	·7	·6	·8
Greater London			
3 Numbers employed in furniture manufacture, thousands	25·8	38·2	63·4
4 Percentage of furniture to all workers	1·8	1·2	1·5
5 Percentage of London furniture workers to England and Wales furniture workers	38·9	37·4	39·2
6 Location Quotient for furniture in Greater London	2·5	2·0	1·8

the first two centres had diminished to insignificance, while the inner East End's share had fallen to 17 per cent. But in compensation certain areas of what can be called the outer East End, or the extension of the Victorian manufacturing belt—Poplar, Hackney, Tottenham, Edmonton, Walthamstow—had almost one-third of the total workers of Greater London. This major shift finds no parallel in the clothing trades.

The directories permit a closer analysis of the major concentrations of the industry. Figures 15–17 show the decline of an important quarter within the West End branch of the industry. This was situated on the borders of the boroughs of Holborn, St Marylebone and St Pancras, and was focussed on Tottenham Court Road and Euston Road/Marylebone Road. (See West End key map, front endpaper.) It advanced a few blocks north of the latter line, into the

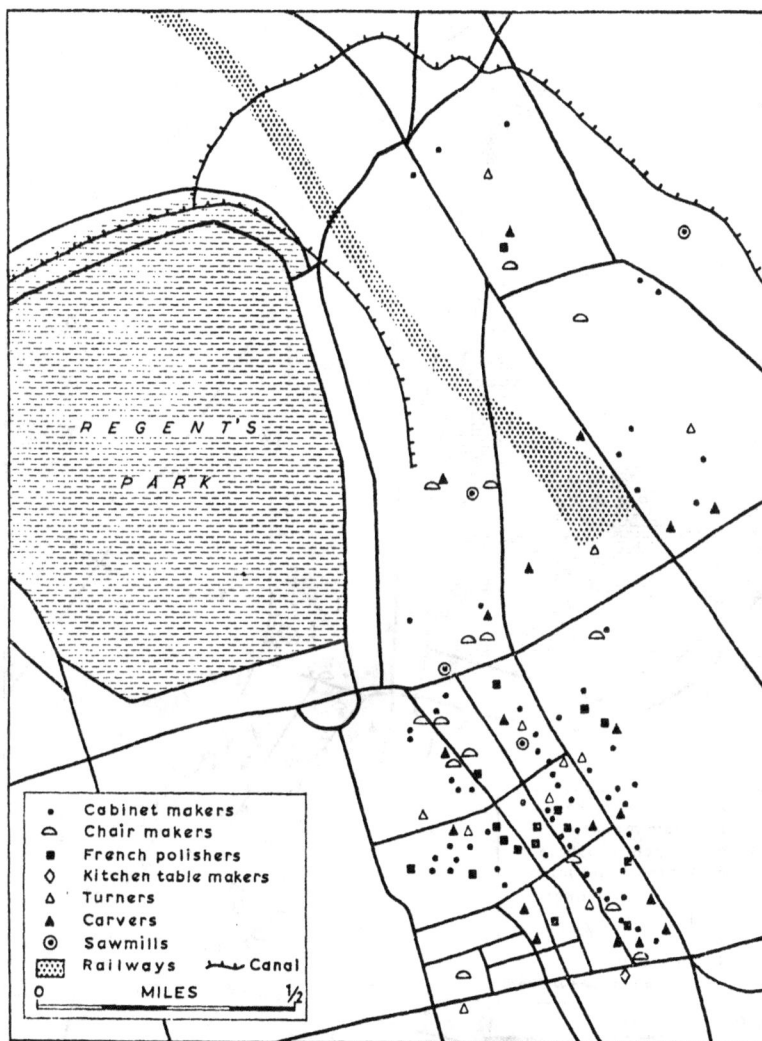

Fig. 15. Furniture: Tottenham Court Road–Camden Town, 1861
(Source: Directories)

Cumberland Market district west of Hampstead Road, but then
stopped quite sharply. By 1951 a few scattered workshops, generally
in mews premises, were the sole remains of this once-flourishing
quarter. The East End quarter has shown greater resilience. Its

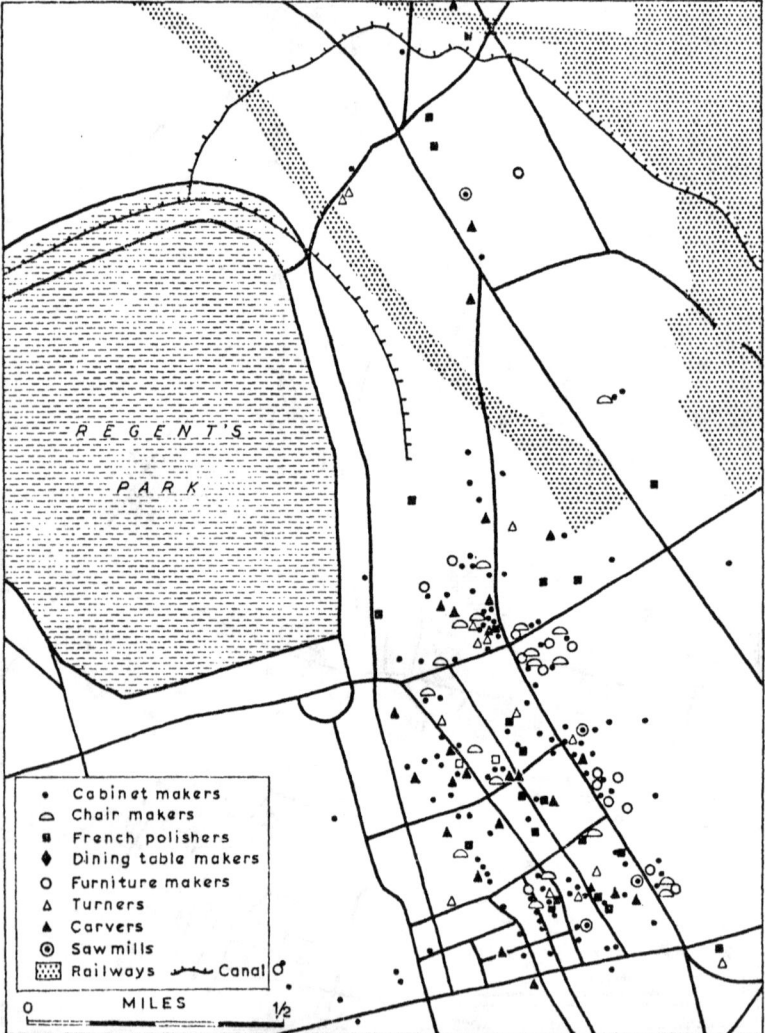

Fig. 16. Furniture: Tottenham Court Road–Camden Town, 1901
(Source: Directories)

fortunes are plotted in Figures 18–20. The map for 1861 shows the quarter firmly centred around the Curtain Road–Old Street district of Shoreditch, at the western edge of that borough. From it cabinet- and chair-makers spread outwards, north of Old Street into

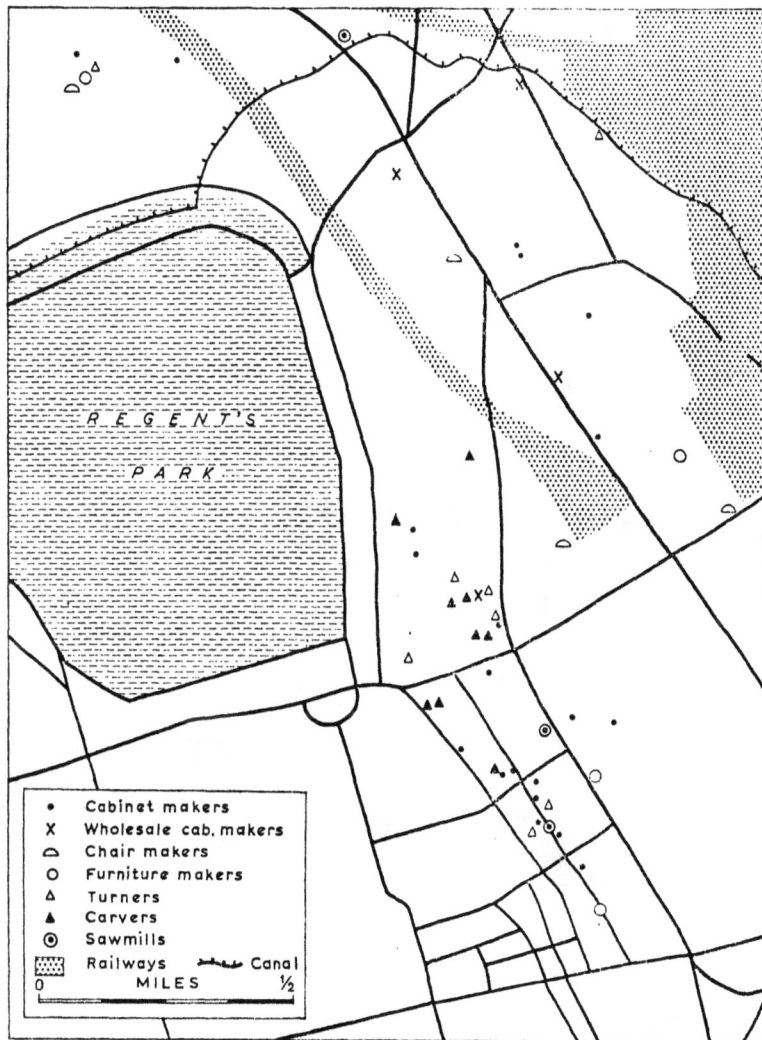

Fig. 17. Furniture: Tottenham Court Road–Camden Town, 1951
(Source: Directories)

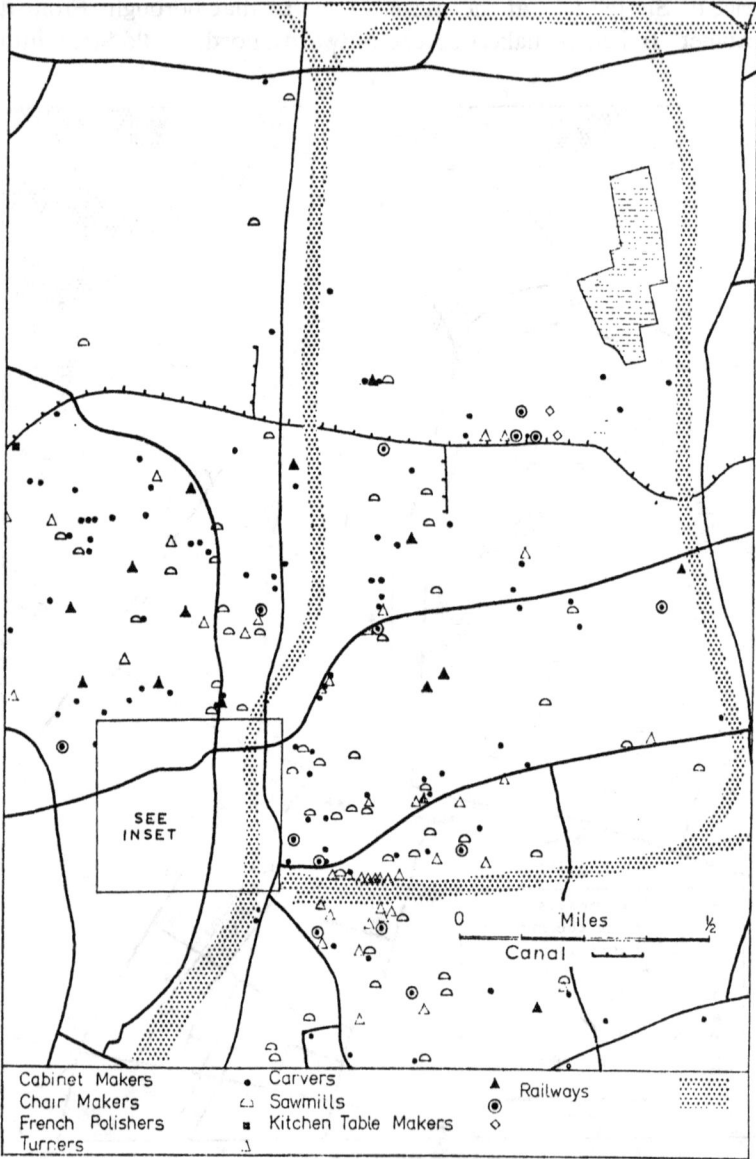

Fig. 18. Furniture: East End, 1861 (Source: Directories)

Hoxton and east of Shoreditch High Street into north-east Shoreditch and western Bethnal Green. They did not extend north of the
Regent's Canal, though some firms were actually located upon it,
especially the sawmills and their associated carvers and turners.
Otherwise sawmills were distributed widely among the furniture-
makers they served. French-polishers alone did not spread widely;
almost without exception they were in the central Curtain Road
area. In 1901 the quarter had spread much more widely eastwards
along Bethnal Green Road and Hackney Road. It had also expanded north of the canal, most notably in Hackney along the
Mare Street axis. This axis now limited the quarter quite sharply to

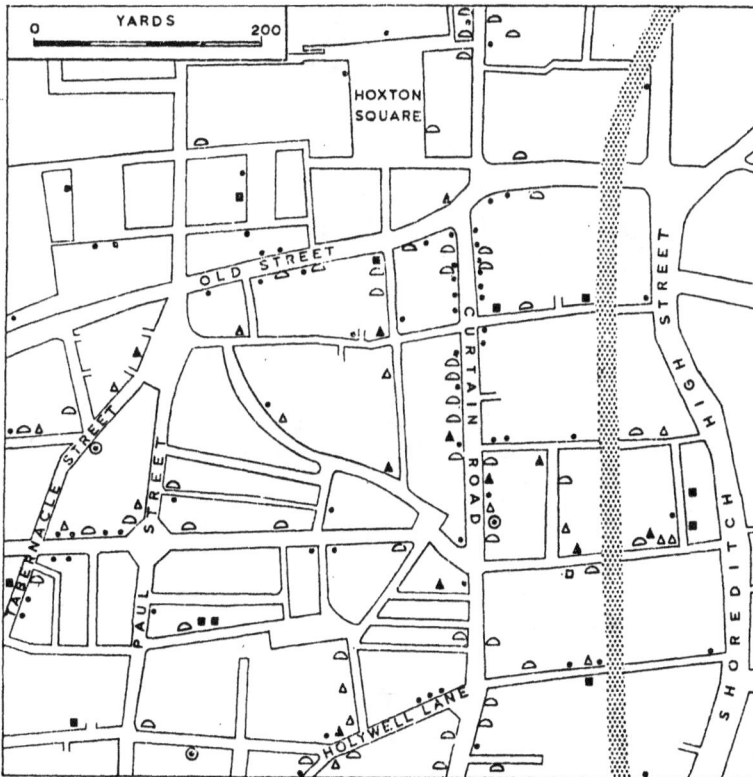

Fig. 18. Inset

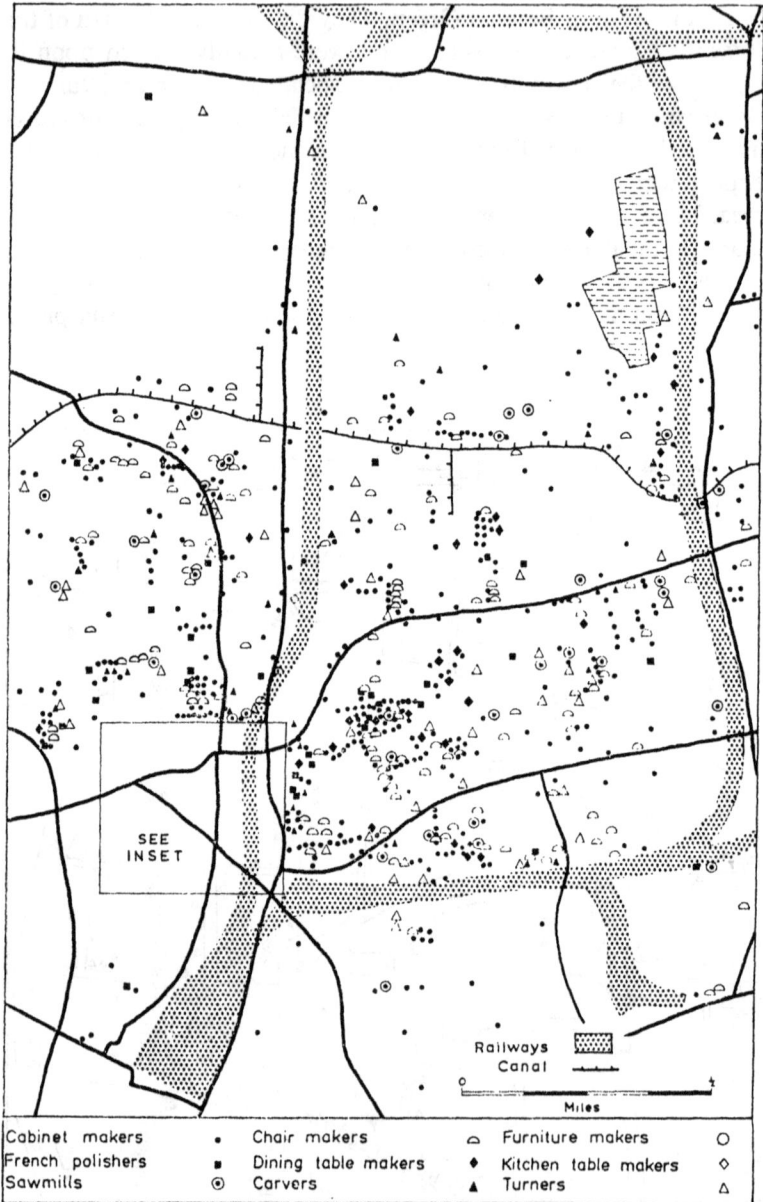

SEE
INSET

Railways
Canal

0   1
Miles

Cabinet makers	•	Chair makers	•	Furniture makers	⌒
French polishers	■	Dining table makers	■	Kitchen table makers	◆
Sawmills	⊙	Carvers	⊙	Turners	▲

Fig. 19. Furniture: East End, 1901 (Source: Directories)

the east. The French-polishers were still distinct in their allegiance to the Curtain Road area. The 1951 map shows the area in slow decline. It probably indeed exaggerates this decline, because the average size of firms has increased and of this fact the directory entries take no account. It is noticeable that very few firms are recorded in Hackney, which was now very important but where the larger firm was probably dominant. Firms styling themselves 'cabinet makers' or 'chair makers' had declined sharply and had been replaced by 'furniture makers'. The French-polishers at last had spread out from a shrunken Curtain Road district, and were fairly widely distributed.

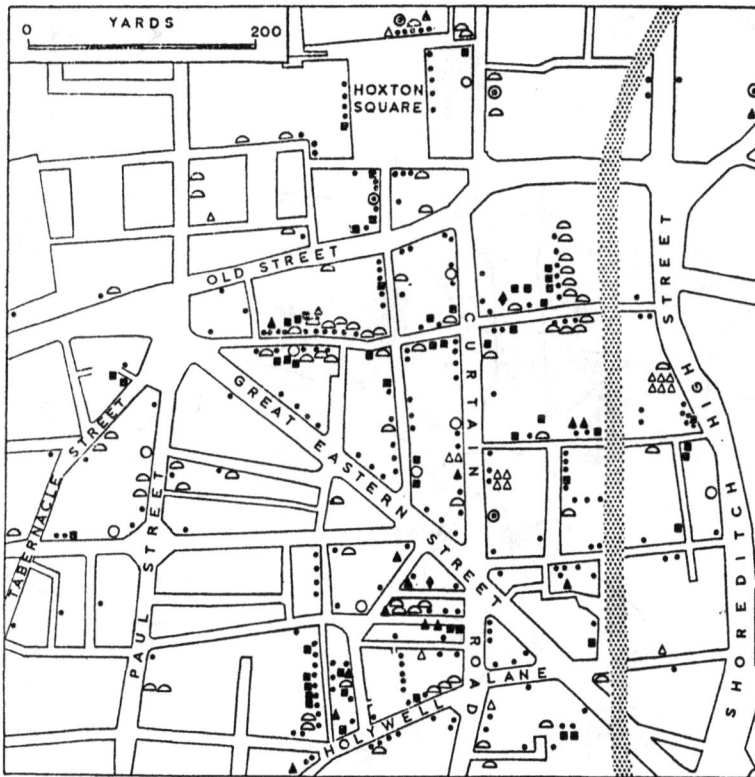

Fig. 19. Inset

Cabinet makers	•	Sawmills	⊛
Wholesale cabinet makers	×	Carvers	▲
Chair makers	◠	Turners	△
Furniture makers	○	Dining table makers	◆
French polishers	■	Kitchen table makers	◇

Fig. 20. Furniture: East End, 1951 (Source: Directories)

TABLE 9

FURNITURE: LOCALIZATION WITHIN LONDON, 1861 AND 1951

(Source: Censuses, 1861 and 1951)

	1861			1951		
	Numbers employed	Percentage of Greater London total	Local Location Quotient	Numbers employed	Percentage of Greater London total	Local Location Quotient
England and Wales	66422			161662		
Greater London	25809	100·0		63377	100·0	
County of London	25101	97·3		35892	56·6	
Westminster M.B.	1940	7·5	0·8	1217	1·9	0·2
St Marylebone M.B.	2200	8·5	1·5	861	1·4	0·4
St Pancras M.B.	3052	11·7	1·9	2205	3·5	1·2
Holborn M.B.	1432	5·6	1·6	658	1·0	0·4
Finsbury M.B.	1854	7·2	1·9	1492	2·4	1·2
Southwark M.B.	1607	6·2	1·2	813	1·3	0·9
Shoreditch M.B.	3928	15·2	4·0	5092	8·0	7·2
Bethnal Green M.B.	2563	9·9	3·2	4040	6·4	11·2
Stepney M.B.	1466	5·7	0·7	1414	2·2	1·0
Poplar M.B.	100	0·4	0·2	2465	3·9	3·0
Hackney M.B.	} 394	} 1·5	} 0·7	{ 4445	7·0	3·9
Stoke Newington M.B.				{ 327	0·5	1·7
Edmonton	116*	0·5	0·3	{ 3480	5·5	6·5
Tottenham				{ 5651	8·9	7·0
Walthamstow	128*	0·5	0·3	2812	4·4	4·4

	1861	1951
Greater London Coefficient of Local Concentration:	0·33	0·45

M.B.—Metropolitan Borough
*—*Not* exact equivalents of 1951 areas

Factors in location

1. *Materials.* The furniture trades differ in one important respect from clothing. Their material can fairly be regarded as a raw material, not a manufactured good (though modern developments, such as plywood, make this statement a qualified one); it tends to be heavy; and save for limited local supplies, such as Chiltern beechwood, it is imported. In the years immediately before the war the industry took half the hardwood and much of the plywood and veneers entering the country.[2] Nearness to a port is therefore an important location factor, and the chief provincial centres—Bristol, Barnstaple, Beith, Leeds—are within easy reach of imported timber. But London is the country's chief port as she is its chief market; and the main concentration of the industry in London is close to the port.

2. *Fuel and power.* Furniture resembles clothing in that it underwent an industrial revolution in the early nineteenth century, which however failed to affect the organization of production or the location of the industry. The circular saw, invented by the Dutch, was used in England from 1777 onwards in shipbuilding;[3] at the end of the eighteenth century came a planing machine; the bandsaw was developed in the early nineteenth century for cutting several thicknesses of wood simultaneously.[4] But the only process which was mechanized to any extent was the heaviest process, the sawing and planing of the planks; and this job came to be undertaken by specialist contractors working in a sawmill for a fixed sum. The process is like that in wholesale clothing, where the wholesaler himself cut the cloth; but in furniture the small master himself arranged for this cutting to be done, and supplied the material. By this time steam was used in the sawmills,[5] and, as the detailed maps of location show, these were often close to water: the East End ones tended to locate along the Regent's Canal. But fuel supplies were certainly not important beyond local siting, as the location of provincial plants makes clear. And soon after this date electric power became widely available to do many jobs formerly done by hand.

3. *Market; labour supplies.* As in clothing, contact with the market proves to have been the primary determining factor in the location of the industry in London. The effect of the market was re-

inforced by the presence of supplies of cheap labour, which tended to produce inertia in location. Once again the market has however had a different significance for different sections of the industry at different times, so that it is necessary to analyse the structure of the industry and the changes in it since 1851.

Four main divisions may be recognized in the London furniture trades.

1. *West End bespoke.* This is the equivalent of that in clothing. But clearly the bespoke system has less point in furniture manufacture than in articles of personal wear, so that it never seems to have been very important save in upholstery, where there was a seasonal demand from the aristocracy during the London season.[6] Even this disappeared after the turn of this century. There is evidence on the other hand that as early as the mid-eighteenth century the best classes of society patronized a warehouse for ready-made furniture —Seddons, in the City—and that this was the normal way of buying furniture of the best sort at that time.[7]

2. *High-class ready-made.* This division of the industry was therefore important at an early date. By the mid-nineteenth century it was centred in the 'trade' (in contradistinction to bespoke) or 'piece-masters' shops, in and around Tottenham Court Road and Euston Road. It is these shops which account for the well-marked West End furniture quarter of the nineteenth century. They seem to have arrived in this area shortly after 1800, coming from St Martin's Lane—a leading centre of the industry in the eighteenth century—probably because of rising rents.[8] The streets in which they settled had for the most part been built up not many years previously.[9]

The characteristic feature of the Tottenham Court Road trade after 1850, however, was the system of contracting for the large retail stores of the area. The piece-master, an upholsterer said:

> . . . has been connected with these large firms. They are men who take a job, generally in a mews, and employ one man, and then they employ a number of boys, whom they get to do what we call the first stuffing in the trade; that is, the interior part of the chair or sofa, putting the springs in, and webbing.[10]

This system could have arisen only after the advent of the large stores themselves, that is after about 1840. The first record of the biggest, John Maple, is in partnership in Tottenham Court Road in 1841; he took over sole control of the business in 1845. Maple, like others, started as a wholesale draper, and apparently came into furniture through upholstery.[11]

At first these stores carried out work in their own workshops, and some perhaps continued to do so, at least in upholstery. But contracting out, or sweating, soon became the rule. In the 80's a witness said:

> I have worked for Messrs Maple; and they have always been, to my mind, the one firm for the cabinet trade who have been the pioneers in the sweating system.[12]

Subcontract was alleged to have existed by 1855 or earlier, but it expanded greatly between 1870 and 1890, when the big shops cut their workshop staffs. By the late 80's Maples said that they bought goods from perhaps a thousand different shops, and (it was claimed) made less than 10 per cent of what they sold.[13]

Whatever may have been the case earlier, by the 80's the Tottenham Court Road workshops worked directly for the big retailer, having established a reputation for a particular specialized article. Maples were said to prefer the practice, because thereby they could set one maker competing in price against another, and indeed against the workmen in Maples' own shops, who might have their wages cut by reference to the piece-master's price.[14]

In their earlier years the big Tottenham Court Road stores had gone fairly wide afield for their goods. Henry Mayhew had claimed in 1861 that the 'black houses, or linen-drapers at the west end of London' got their goods chiefly from Clerkenwell, where according to him the practices of subcontract and division of labour had developed as early as 1820.[15] In the 80's the head of Maples confirmed this:

> Do you know what kind of work is made at the East-end, in Bethnal Green, and Curtain-road?
> . . . years ago, in our early days, we used to have to buy a lot of that description of low-class furniture, but now we have no demand for it.[16]

By that time Maples ordered and paid weekly, so rapid execution of orders was the rule, and it had become extremely important for the small workshop to be located close to the store. Those who gave evidence about Maples' practices to the Select Committee on the Sweating System were seldom more than ten minutes' walk from the store.[17] Thus a tightly-knit industrial quarter developed.

The Tottenham Court Road had a transitional character. On the one hand the systems of subcontract and division of labour were carried through to a high degree. But on the other hand the product was of high quality; Maple described it as 'the medium class and up to the very highest classes of furniture',[18] though the former rather than the latter probably predominated. A trade guide of the 80's said:

> The chief upholsterers and furniture-makers are particular about their workmen, and it is not easy to procure work at Gillowe's, Jackson and Graham's, and houses of their standing.[19]

When it was investigated by the Committee in the late 80's the Tottenham Court Road trade was at its zenith. It must have begun to decline after 1900, and sharply between the two wars. As will be seen, during this period the more successful manufacturers were expanding and turning to full-scale factory production. In this area, where rents were constantly rising because of the pressure of the central business district of the West End, it was impossible to expand *in situ*. Bombing and slum clearance have dealt a further blow to the industry since 1939. Today it survives only in the workshops attached to the stores, notably Maples, and a few surviving small masters' shops tucked away obscurely in mews premises behind the main roads.

3. *The East End ready-made trade*. Historically this was the most important division of the London furniture trades, and here the systems of subcontract and division of labour were carried to the furthest possible extent. Of all the divisions this was the most varied and complex. It embraced the skilled cabinet-maker who might make bespoke goods for a rich customer of Maples, or first-class ready-made goods for the large retail stores of Tottenham Court Road or the City. But its more typical method of production was that described by a skilled cabinet-maker to the Select Committee on Sweating:

I have taken the trouble to walk round about Bethnal Green, where some of these garret masters' dens are, late at night, after I have done my own day's work. . . . I saw a man and three boys, each of these boys was under 16 years of age, making a common mahogany chest of drawers. Now the ordinary way in which we put chests of drawers together is, that we dove-tail one piece of wood into the other; but there was no dove-tailing in this; only what we call Birmingham dove-tails, that is, nails . . .[20]

This grade of product was already typical of the London trade by 1844, when a guide to London's iniquities warned the unsuspecting stranger:

You may now furnish a good-sized house with commodities all new for thirty pounds; but you must make up your mind never to sit upon the chairs, use the tables, or lie upon the beds.[21]

The *raison d'être* of the whole system, of course, was the poverty of the market:

But there is a demand, is there not, for the paltry rubbish as you call it on the part of the public?
Yes, there is a sale for it no doubt; there must be, or they would not go on producing it.[22]

Like the sweated clothing trade, this was a wholesale system, founded on close contact between the wholesaler and a host of small manufacturers. The small-master system flourished in the East End furniture because (as again in clothing) the industrial revolution in the trade did not substantially increase the amount of capital needed to start up an enterprise. As seen already, the only process requiring expensive mechanical equipment was the sawing and planing of the planks, and soon after 1850 the system developed of contracting this work out to specialists in a sawmill. So that in the 80's

. . . a pound's worth of tools and a second pound in cash starts many 'cabinet-makers' on the career of independent worker, and double that amount will often convert him into an employer.[23]

The small-master system thus became entrenched in the East End trade, and methods of production described in the Booth Survey were still substantially unchanged when the Working Party on Furniture reported in 1946.

Although it was easy to enter the trade, the lack of apprenticeship prevented a complete education in it. The three basic features of the East End system were: the wholesale system of trade; the small-master system of production; and the specialization of process. Together these features determined the structure and location of the industry.

In the heyday of the trade, when the Booth Survey described it, the origin of the whole productive process lay in the wholesale dealers, who were located in the small area around Curtain Road, Great Eastern Street and the adjacent streets east of Shoreditch High Street and south of Old Street. The zone of warehouses extended westwards and southwards into the metropolitan borough of Finsbury, but most of the East End furniture went through the dealers in the immediate neighbourhood of Curtain Road.[24] Like the wholesale clothiers of the Houndsditch area, the Curtain Road dealers were originally City men. Indeed, actual furniture manufacture remained in the City until well into the nineteenth century, when rising rents drove them out. J. L. Oliver has used directory material to analyse the move from the City. In 1800, 13 furniture firms were recorded in the City; in 1859, eight. Curtain Road and its neighbourhood in 1801 had only one firm; in 1859, 51. Curtain Road was still mainly residential in 1809, but already had timber yards, turnery and chair works. In 1832 it was passing over rapidly to manufacturing and commerce. The building of Broad Street and Liverpool Street stations in the 60's and 70's displaced firms into Curtain Road.[25]

The Curtain Road dealers were simply middlemen, selling, as a witness put it to the Committee on Sweating, to firms 'in this end of the town', or to country dealers.[26] These firms had a lucrative export market. In 1888 nearly three-quarters of a million pounds' worth of furniture was exported, nearly a third of it to Australia, much of the rest to South Africa, the Argentine and the United States.[27] East End manufacture was done to the express order of the dealer; a maker would produce for stock only when times were slack, and might have to hawk the goods thus made along Curtain

Road on Saturday morning.[28] In certain cases the dealer even provided the raw material, as in the clothing trades.[29]

The usual process of production was as follows. Having in normal times delivered his order to the Curtain Road dealer on the Saturday, and received another for completion by the weekend following, the manufacturer—a chair-maker, for instance—would first go, on Monday morning, to the small timber merchant near to his workshop, where he would buy the necessary timber with his last week's earnings. Many of the timber merchants might give a week's credit, but the final result was the same: the maker must sell on Saturday to pay on Monday, hence the need to hawk when his goods had not been made to order. The timber bought by the maker had come from the importer through a large merchant to the small one; but the last filled a vital need in the East End trade in that he

> will in any case sell to them in very small quantities, in the same way that the housewife with small means and irregular income is obliged to patronize the small 'general shop' in her own street.[30]

The timber would be bought in planks ready for 'marking out'. This done, it was secondly taken to a sawyer who hired space in a nearby sawmill. Turning and fret-cutting might also be done, if necessary, by other specialist workers in the same mill. Thirdly, any carving to be done was again, as a rule, contracted out to a specialist. Thus the work done by the chair-maker himself was limited to planing, shaping, dowelling, glueing, cleaning-up and glass-papering. The chair frames were then returned 'in the white', that is to say, unpolished and unupholstered, to the wholesale warehouse, and were kept there until ordered from the dealer by the retailer or the provincial dealer. At this point the upholstering and polishing were usually subcontracted, the French-polishing quite commonly being separately given out by the contracting upholsterer, or alternatively done by a nomadic polisher in the dealer's warehouse.[31]

This pattern of extreme vertical disintegration of manufacture, depending on a wholesale system of distribution, might be repeated for any of the East End furniture trades of the 80's. It was paralleled at High Wycombe, where a trade in cheap chairs had arisen after 1830, and was producing by the late 80's over a million chairs a year to compete with the products of the East End small masters.[32] Indeed it seems a natural response to the conditions of production of cheap goods by imperfectly trained labour with limited capital equipment. But it was made possible only after 1850, through the development of sawing for the trade by tenants in the mills. The Booth Survey said in 1888:

> Thirty years ago 'the Road' was almost entirely made up of workshops, and the differentiation of the dealer and maker has been going on rapidly during the past fifteen years.[33]

The small-master system received a powerful impetus in the 80's from the immigration of green Russian and Polish labour. Less Jewish labour went into furniture than into clothing, but it did achieve an important place for itself in certain specialized lines of cheap-furniture production such as bedroom suites, duchesse tables and pedestal tables, which were always in demand in 'the Road'.[34] By 1900 it was alleged that East End immigrant labour was competing with skilled West End cabinet-makers in

> Not the very cheap, but . . . middle-class furniture, bedroom suites, that the ordinary better-paid artisan would use and the ordinary tradesman would buy . . . that mostly goes into the front shops of many West End and provincial firms.[35]

The presence of the Jewish labour pool undoubtedly strengthened the East End system economically. But it was not the primary factor in the evolution of that system, which indeed dates from a period long before the main immigration. The primary factor was the technical one: the limited amount of capital necessary, linked with the wholesale system of production and the presence of cheap unskilled labour in the East End, of which the Jewish immigrants formed only a part.

The separation of making from wholesaling took place rapidly between 1860 and 1900. At that latter date, as the detailed distribution maps show, the process was not complete, for cabinet-making had not entirely deserted Shoreditch. But the 1901 map shows the truth of the statement in the Booth Survey, a few years earlier, that 'Bethnal Green does hardly anything but make':[36] the

French-polishers, who were ancillary to the wholesalers, were hardly found there at all. Only in 1951 had the wholesale cabinet-makers and their ancillaries reached Bethnal Green in significant numbers.

4. *The factory trade.* Since 1900 the production of furniture for a mass market has continued to expand, stimulated after 1920 by the introduction on a large scale of plywood, which cheapened production. This expansion has however been accompanied by a revolution in the organization of the trade: relatively, the small-master system has suffered great losses at the expense of the factory system of production. The reason for this is technical. There has been a rapid application of machinery to a wide range of processes, aided by electrification after 1900. The large factory alone can economically install and use the full range of equipment now available. The formerly important East End footwear industry also faced such a technical challenge, and declined as a result. But, unlike the London shoemaker, the London furniture-maker has managed to adapt himself with conspicuous success to this new form of organization.

The incipient factory could already be seen in the East End trade when the Booth Survey studied it. There were then three or four works with over 50 men each, selling direct to the Tottenham Court Road shops, the provinces and the colonies. Already the largest was Lebus, in Tabernacle Street. It was Lebus who pioneered the move outwards to space in the suburbs by moving to Tottenham, before the year 1903.[37] Between the wars many firms in Shoreditch and Bethnal Green followed suit. Bluestone and Elvin went from Shoreditch to Walthamstow in 1928; B. and I. Nathan from Curtain Road to Hackney and then in 1930 to Edmonton; Beautility from Bethnal Green to Edmonton in the mid–30's. Since 1945, partly because of government encouragement, a few have gone farther out. Jarman and Platt went from Bethnal Green to Romford, about 1955; Hille from Shoreditch to Lea Bridge Road and then to St. Albans; and Greaves and Thomas (Put-U-Up), who had moved from Shoreditch to Clapton as early as 1911, out to Harlow New Town in 1954.[38]

But the economies of factory production were not ineluctable, as is proved by the number of medium—and even small—scale firms which survive in the trade. The 1951 Census of Production showed that (including working proprietors) the average establishment in furniture and upholstery in the United Kingdom had 28·1 workers. The 1851 Census returns for cabinet-makers and chair-makers gave 5·1 workers per firm in England and Wales, assuming that at that time all proprietors were working. In 1851 over 90 per cent of the firms with over 60 per cent of the workers had less than 10 workers. By 1951 the figures were 60 per cent of firms and nearly 10 per cent of workers, while just over half the workers were in plants with less than 100 workers.[39] The factory revolution in furniture, then, has not been by any means complete. And almost certainly the small-master system has remained most firmly entrenched in London. Munby's description of the furniture trades in the inner East End in 1951[40] accords almost precisely with that of Aves for the Booth Survey in 1888, save for the substitution of spray painting for French-polishing and the appearance of veneering as a separate craft. For the East End, then, the verdict of the Booth Survey still holds good:

> . . . machinery for these . . . processes is rarely set up in a market in which workers are so numerous and labour so cheap as in the East End of London. There, the small system prevails, and there are no signs that it will not continue to hold its own against the large system that would have to take its place if all the . . . processes were ordinarily done by machinery.[41]

A more decided change in the organization of the furniture trade since 1890 has been the decline of the wholesale function. Already the Booth Survey noted 'the increasing extent to which retailers and provincial dealers are buying direct from East End makers'.[42] But this process gained added force in the present century from better communications, especially from the spread of the telephone, and from the greater capital and experience of even the small East End workshops. Clearly the big factories would sell direct; but by 1946 the Working Party thought that the wholesaler exaggerated his importance to the small maker also.[43] The Census of Production in 1950 showed that 73·5 per cent of total production went direct to retailers, only 4 per cent through a wholesaler at all.[44] It seems almost certain therefore that many of the East End firms describing themselves as wholesale cabinet-makers in 1951 were in fact manufacturing cabinet-makers who acted as their own wholesalers, distributing direct to retailers. The fact that by this date their distribution so closely resembles that of the ordinary furniture-makers goes to support this view.

It is safe to conclude then that nearness to the Curtain Road wholesaler was no longer a factor of importance in the location of the furniture industry by the interwar period. The attractive force of the immigrant-labour pool was now far weaker, as second-generation descendants spread out of the East End. Despite this the Board of Trade found that between 1933 and 1938, out of 198 furniture works established in the country, no less than 126 were within the Greater London area;[45] and the Census figures for 1951 show clearly enough that the industry has not migrated far from its traditional home. The reasons are simple. By the interwar period the furniture industry was no longer an export industry. But after 1918 the importance of the port for export was replaced by that of the enormous home market in the London region itself, and of the region's road network for distribution over a wider area. Furniture is easily scratched and thus not well suited to rail transport, with its inevitable trans-shipments; but in the 1200-cubic-foot van it found an ideal means of distribution. The other reason for the continued concentration in the East End was simple inertia. As small workshops expanded into medium—and even large—scale factories they simply moved to the nearest possible site where there was fairly cheap land for expansion. Thereby they might hope to keep their existing skilled labour force together, and continue to enjoy the advantages of the London market. There was no reason to do otherwise. At any rate up till about 1925 cheap land was readily available only a few miles north of Shoreditch and Bethnal Green, on the Lea Valley marshes; and here the firms naturally gravitated. This process will be analysed in more detail in Chapter 8.

Victorian London contained three great manufacturing industries which were distinctively East End trades: clothing, furniture and the now much-decayed footwear industry (which is not considered in detail here).[46] These three trades had in common three basic features, which go far to explain their pattern of location. They produced a consumer good whose sale was exceptionally liable to vagaries of season or fashion; hence they must locate near to their final market.

They sold through a wholesaler, whose presence obviated the need for the manufacturer to tie up money in working capital; this wholesaler had originated in the financial centre of the City of London, he remained located at the edge of the City, and hence the manufacturer must have his plant close by. They were assembly industries where the advantages of mechanization were not apparent; they tended to substitute cheap unskilled labour for capital equipment, and hence drew on the vast reservoir of such labour in the East End of London.

In all three trades since 1900 the last two features have become less apparent than they were, while even the first has lost some of its force because of the speed of modern communication. The changes which have taken place have however been very different in degree from one industry to another. In footwear, the industry has gone over most completely to mechanized factory production; the London manufacturer has failed to adapt himself to the change, and the trade has largely left the capital for the provinces. In furniture the change has been less complete, and in so far as it has occurred it has occurred to the same extent in London as elsewhere; consequently there has been an internal shift of location within the Greater London area, but one of small magnitude, towards sites suitable for factory production. In the great complex of the clothing trades the degree of change has been greater in some branches than in others. In certain lines, such as men's bespoke clothing, provincial factory production has gained over the London workshop, though London has not failed entirely to mechanize; in others, such as women's outerwear, the small workshop in the traditional quarter of inner London has remained viable because of the importance of close contact with the market. The demands of the market on the one hand, and of technical organization on the other, have done a great deal to influence the changing location of these trades; but the accident of the historical moment, the ability or the failure of manufacturers as a whole to respond to opportunities of change, have proved of literally vital importance to their fortunes in London.

1 Colin Clark, *The Conditions of Economic Progress* (1957), 465. In this table the income elasticity of demand for furniture is in 11 cases above unity and in only three cases below it. See also R. Stone, *The Role of Measurement in Economics* (Cambridge 1951), table 4,

which gives 1·62 for house furniture and floor coverings and 1·27 for house furniture and equipment.

2 Board of Trade, *Working Party Report: Furniture* (H.M.S.O. 1946), 7.

3 S. Smiles, *Industrial Biography: Iron Workers and Tool Makers* (1863), 165–6, claims that the first English sawmill was installed in 1663, but was abandoned due to the hostility of workmen. A second was installed at Limehouse in 1767, destroyed by the mob, but replaced.

4 The account of technical development is based on Working Party Report, op. cit., 83–4.

5 In an Oxford Street works for instance: J. H. Pollen in G. Phillips Bevan, *British Manufacturing Industries* (1876), 132–3.

6 *R. C. Labour, Minutes, Group C*, Q. 8034, *P.P.* 1892, XXXV.

7 R. Edwards and M. Jourdain, *Georgian Cabinet Makers* (1944), 8–10.

8 A. Heal, *The London Furniture Makers from the Restoration to the Victorian Era, 1600–1840* (1953), *passim*. A pioneer in Tottenham Court Road (Lock M.) is recorded 1752, but addresses there became common only post-1800.

9 L.C.C. *Survey of London*, XXI, *Tottenham Court Road and Neighbourhood* (St Pancras, part III) (1949), *passim*. Just south of Euston Road the streets date from 1770–1800, e.g. Maple Street 1777–8, Fitzroy Street 1790.

10 *S. C. Sweating System, Minutes*, Q. 4527, *P.P.* 1888, XX.

11 A. Heal, op. cit., 111.

12 S. C. Sweating System, op. cit., Q. 3922.

13 Ibid., Q. 2135, 2143, 2257–9, 6263–4; *R. C. Labour, Minutes*, Q. 19753, *P.P.* 1892, XXXVI, part II.

14 S. C. Sweating System, op. cit., Q. 4386–7, 4529.

15 H. Mayhew, *London Labour and the London Poor* (1861), III, 223–5.

16 S. C. Sweating System, op. cit., Q. 6160. Also 7243–4. But Lebus said he made a lot for Maples: Q. 7757–8.

17 Ibid., 7705–6. Harrison worked in Little Edward Street, just north of Euston Road. See also Q. 2323, 2436.

18 Ibid., Q. 6160.

19 H. L. Williams, *The Worker's Industrial Index to London* (1881), 14.

20 S. C. Sweating System, op. cit., Q, 2864.

21 Father North, *The Mysteries of London and Stranger's Guide* (1844), 46.

22 *S. C. Emigration and Immigration (Foreigners), Minutes 1889*, Q. 1394, *P.P.* 1889, X. Compare E. Aves in C. Booth (ed.), *Life and Labour of the People in London* (1892–7), IV, 190–1, 213.

23 E. Aves, ibid., 171.

24 Ibid., 160–2.

25 J. L. Oliver, 'In and Out of Curtain Road', *Furniture Record*, 155 (1959), 663, 667.

26 S. C. Sweating System, op. cit., Q. 3227, 3231.

27 Ibid., Q. 32060, *P.P.* 1889, XIV, part I.

28 E. Aves, op. cit., 175–6.

29 This was done in the 60's: *Appendix Fifth Report Children's Employ-*

ment Commissioners, 197, *P.P.* 1866, XXIV. For the 90's in Leeds, R. C. Labour, op. cit., Q. 20031–3. Maples did it: S. C. Sweating System, op. cit., Q. 2375–82.

30 E. Aves, op. cit., 167–8.

31 Ibid., 164–5, 182–6.

32 Ibid., 180; *Annual Report Chief Inspector of Factories*, 1885, 19–21, *P.P.* 1886, XIV.

33 E. Aves, ibid., 187.

34 Ibid., 210; S. C. Sweating System, op. cit., Q. 4594–6.

35 *R. C. Alien Immigration, Minutes*, Q. 14010–11, *P.P.* 1903, IX.

36 E. Aves, op. cit., 158.

37 Ibid., 172; S. C. Sweating System, op. cit., Q. 3787; J. L. Oliver, op. cit., 667. In 1903 a union man alleged that 90 per cent of their Tottenham labour force was green immigrant labour. R. C. Alien Immigration, op. cit., Q. 13990–3.

38 J. L. Oliver, ibid., 668–7; *The Golden Jubilee of Greaves and Thomas Ltd, 1905–1955*.

39 *Census 1851*, Summary Tables, XXX, *P.P.* 1852–3, LXXXVIII, part I; *Census of Production 1951*, vol. 10.

40 D. L. Munby, *Industry and Planning in Stepney* (Oxford 1951), 269–71.

41 E. Aves, op. cit., 190.

42 Ibid., 186.

43 Working Party Report, op. cit., 142.

44 *Census of Production 1950*, vol. 10. But this analysis excluded the smallest firms (one-tenth of the total) which were most likely to sell through a wholesaler.

45 Working Party Report, op. cit., 49–50. This was an area larger than the conurbation.

46 I discuss it elsewhere. P. G. Hall, 'The East London Footwear Industry: An Industrial Quarter in Decline', *East London Papers*, 5 (1962).

6

THE OLDER INDUSTRIES: PRINTING

OF THE old-established London trades, none has been so richly documented from its very origin as printing. It is, therefore, possible in this chapter, unlike the previous chapters, to study in some detail the evolution of a distinctly metropolitan trade in the centuries before the relatively recent period since 1861. In this way we may perhaps gain an insight into the way in which such an industry has grown up in response to the market forces of a capital city.

Distinctions in quality do exist in printing, but they are less apparent than in the trades so far discussed. It is more useful to divide the trade into sections which relate horizontally: newspaper and periodical printing; job and general printing; book work; government work; and the special branches of lithographic printing, and of engraving with its related techniques. For all these branches the same factors of location have their effect, but their relative force varies from one branch to another. After a brief survey of the facts of location for the trade as a whole, the forces influencing location will be analysed for the most important divisions.

Facts of location

In Table 10 the statistics for 1861 may be understated because ancillary workers are probably not included. But making all possible allowance for this fact, it is clear that since 1861 the printing industry has expanded very greatly, both in England and Wales and in London. The trend was already apparent in the 90's, when the Booth Survey commented: 'The growth of the trade has, however, been enormous everywhere.'[1] The industry is markedly concentrated in London but the degree of concentration has diminished: in 1861 over half the country's printers were in London, in 1951 a little over two-fifths. Between 1921 and 1951 however the proportion remained relatively stable, though London's Location Quotient fell because its proportion of all workers was rising.

TABLE 10

PRINTING: ENGLAND AND WALES,

GREATER LONDON, 1861, 1921, 1951

(Source: Censuses, 1861, 1921, 1951)

	1861	1921	1951
England and Wales			
1 Numbers employed in printing, thousands	49·6	242·4	307·8
2 Percentage of printing to all workers	0·5	1·4	1·5
Greater London			
3 Numbers employed in printing, thousands	26·5	108·8	135·2
4 Percentage of printing to all workers	1·8	3·4	3·2
5 Percentage of London printing workers to England and Wales printing workers	53·4	44·9	43·9
6 Location Quotient for printing in Greater London	3·4	2·4	2·0

The main facts about the location of the industry within London are set out in Table 11. The 1861 figures show a noticeably centralized pattern of location. Six central areas—Westminster, Holborn, the City, Finsbury, Shoreditch, Southwark—contained 57 per cent of the printers of Greater London. This figure is however almost certainly an understatement because it is based on place-of-residence tables, and printers, like clerical workers, seem to have started to move their homes out of central London even by 1861. The Booth Survey thirty years later wrote that 'few of the men live near their work'; they spread widely through the suburbs, with one or two notable concentrations:

> ... in Walworth, south of the Thames, and in the neighbour-hood of the Caledonian Road on the north, a regular colony of printers existing in each place. The men who live in these

D

districts generally walk to their work, convenience of situation, with this aim in view, being a principal factor in the choice of residence.[2]

This fact explains the important concentrations of printers which already existed in 1861 in St Pancras (8 per cent of the London total), Islington (over 7 per cent) and Lambeth (over 6 per cent). Commuting movements in Victorian London were such that the St Pancras printers almost certainly went for the most part to Westminster, the Islington ones to Finsbury and the City, and those from Lambeth to Southwark. Their addition would make the 1861 total for the central area almost 80 per cent.

By the time of the Booth Survey some printers were already living farther afield. The cheap fares of the Great Eastern Railway were drawing some through Liverpool Street to Tottenham, Edmonton and Walthamstow. But many remained faithful to the inner suburbs, the New Survey reported in 1930.[3] The 1931 place-of-residence tables show that over one-fifth of the printers were still living in the four metropolitan boroughs of Islington, Hackney, Lambeth and Camberwell. This is a measure of the continuing centralization of the industry itself. In 1951 the six central areas mentioned above contained 61 per cent of the total printers (as against the 57 per cent enumerated as living there in 1861). Of these just over 40 per cent were in the City and Westminster alone. The greatest relative concentrations were in Shoreditch and Southwark, where printers were proportionally over three times as important as in London as a whole.

The 1951 statistics also permit analysis of location of two divisions within the trade: newspaper and periodical work; and other sorts of printing (principally book and general work). Newspaper and periodical printing is as might be supposed very highly centralized. Almost exactly half the country's workers were in Greater London and of those 70 per cent worked in the City and in Westminster (the City 51 per cent, Westminster 19 per cent). In other sorts of printing London's share of the national total dropped to 41 per cent and of the London total only 27 per cent was in the City and Westminster, 51 per cent in the six central areas.

The printing industry therefore is distinctly a central-area industry. Unlike the East End trades, competition of commerce

TABLE 11

PRINTING: LOCALIZATION WITHIN LONDON, 1861 AND 1951

(Source: Censuses, 1861 and 1951)

	1861			1951		
	Numbers employed	Percentage of Greater London total	Local Location Quotient	Numbers employed	Percentage of Greater London total	Local Location Quotient
England and Wales	49600			307754		
Greater London	26504	100·0		135186	100·0	
County of London	25979	98·0		108594	80·3	
Westminster M.B.	2528	9·5	1·0	21536	15·9	1·5
Holborn M.B.	2040	7·7	2·3	6950	5·1	2·2
Finsbury M.B.	3143	11·9	3·1	7439	5·5	2·9
City	2940	11·1	2·8	33312	24·5	3·1
Shoreditch M.B.	1813	6·8	1·8	5710	4·2	3·6
Southwark M.B.	2637	10·0	1·9	7322	5·4	3·6
St Pancras M.B.	2214	8·4	1·3	4804	3·6	1·3
Islington M.B.	1909	7·2	1·6	2238	1·7	0·8
Lambeth M.B.	1758	6·6	1·4	3224	2·4	1·0

Greater London Coefficient of Local Concentration:

1861	1951
0·34	0·37

M.B.—Metropolitan Borough

for sites has forced its workers out to suburban homes. But they have moved to the inner rather than the outer suburbs.

Factors in location

The rapid expansion of the printing industry since 1861 is explained by the spread of literacy, first to the commercial and professional middle class which arose out of the Industrial Revolution and secondly, after the Forster Act of 1870, to the working classes. Two ancillary pieces of legislation were of considerable importance in hastening this literacy: the Act of 1839 establishing the penny post, which led to a greatly increased circulation of printed material; and the repeal of the newspaper stamp duty in 1855, which added the penny press to the penny post as boons of Victorian civilization.

The two features of the location of the industry are, first, that much of the country's printing is done in London; second, that much of London's printing is done in central London. Clearly there are common factors behind these two tendencies. Actually the location of the industry represents a state of uneasy equilibrium between two opposed forces: one attracting the industry towards central London, the other attracting it into the suburbs or provinces. But the relative strength of the two forces varies from one branch of the trade to another. The most conspicuous contrast is between newspaper and government printing, on the one hand, and book printing on the other. Job and general printing may be regarded as intermediate between these two.

1. *Book production*. Caxton was a book printer, and for at least a century after him printing was almost invariably book work. From the start London became the centre of book production in this country. Caxton himself set up his press close by Westminster Abbey, but in terms of later history this was a false start; almost immediately afterwards the printers gravitated towards the City. First foreigners like John Lettou and William de Machlinia began to print law books near the Inns of Court. Then general book printers moved too: Wynkyn de Worde, Caxton's apprentice, went in 1500 from Westminster to Fleet Street; Julian Notary from Westminster to Temple Bar in 1502; Richard Pynson from outside Temple Bar to Fleet Street about the same time. The main source of attraction was St Paul's Cathedral. Book production began

where the old medieval manuscripts had been sold—the precincts of the cathedral or parish church. In London the merchants' church with its rich market proved superior to the royal church of Westminster, and in the course of the sixteenth century St Paul's Churchyard itself, Paternoster Row and Fleet Street became the centre of the trade. Within the Churchyard space was already at a premium in Tudor times and printers began to hive off the manufacturing process to cheaper sites towards the edge of the City, leaving only a small retail shop near the Cathedral. Thus Fleet Street became the printing quarter of London.[4]

From 1586 until the end of the seventeenth century London's hegemony in English printing was secured by a law prohibiting provincial printing except for the university presses. After this law became a dead letter Fleet Street was powerful enough to retain its supremacy, and printers coming to London to set up in business were naturally attracted there. Thus the founder of the house of Spottiswoode settled on what was then the edge of the printing quarter, in New Street Square between Fetter Lane and Shoe Lane, in 1753. At that time this area was still residential, but in the following century and a half the workshops expanded to cover the whole triangular area bounded by New Street Square, Little New Street and Shoe Lane.[5] The history of Harrisons provides an especially instructive case. Here the founder came from Reading to take up apprenticeship in the City in 1738. His first business was in Warwick Lane. Later in the eighteenth century the firm was in Paternoster Row. But Harrisons became government printers, and in 1801 were pioneer emigrants from the City to Westminster, when they settled in the Strand in order to be near the government departments which supplied their copy. The firm has remained in this area ever since. It settled finally in 1840 in St Martin's Lane and has subsequently expanded *in situ* by taking over neighbouring sites as they fell vacant. Now it has large works also at Hayes and High Wycombe.[6]

Up to 1850 then there was a simple rule of location for book printing. Its vital raw material was its copy, and this arrived in the centre of the metropolis. A large part of its market might also be found there. Before the arrival of modern communications no real choice of location was possible. Pressure of rents might force the industry from the most accessible and commanding positions on to less valuable sites, but space was not a considerable problem because the industry was not yet mechanized and remained small in scale. Editions were small and machines, it was thought, could not produce the finer work.

For the humble job printer the situation was similar. Up to 1850 a primitive hand machine was commonly used. The first practicable treadle machine was invented in the United States in 1851 and improved versions began to sweep the English market in the 60's.[7] But these machines were designed for the small master, and permitted the jobbing trade to remain small in scale. Consequently pressure of space in central London was not serious. At the beginning of the nineteenth century half the printing works of what was then London lay within the City. In 1855 the London Society of Compositors' guide to printing offices listed 423 in all, of which 158 were bounded by the line Blackfriars Bridge—St Paul's —Smithfield—Holborn—Drury Lane—Charing Cross—Strand— Blackfriars. Most of the large firms (large, that is, by the standards of the day) remained here too.[8] Even in the 90's the Booth Survey found the greatest concentration of bookbinders within half a mile of Holborn Viaduct. The reason, as an employment guide of the same period found, was that City bookbinding was predominantly commercial: red-tape binding, eyeletting and the like.[9]

This was the state of equilibrium in 1850, and for some branches of the printing trade—commercial jobbing for example—it would not easily change. The average firm has remained too small, too dependent on the immediate demands of the market, to move very far from it. The incomplete return for England and Wales in the 1851 Census gave the average firm in printing and bookbinding 7·4 workers. By 1951 the size of the average establishment in printing and bookbinding (except newspapers and periodicals) was still only 31·3.[10] The small workshop was economically viable, here as in East End clothing, because the technical revolution that occurred in the trade failed to increase substantially the amount of capital needed to enter it. Such a workshop adapted itself to the fierce competition for land in central London by finding obscure, often unsuitable, premises, and adapting itself to conditions as best it might. In the 60's there were said to be many offices more than 50 years old in converted houses or in sheds in backyards,[11] and thirty years after that a trade witness could say:

I will not say at the present time—but up till recently any hole or corner seemed to be good enough for small printing offices, either at the top of the house or in the basement . . . An improvement has taken place, especially in the larger offices, but there is still a deal to be done in making the offices more healthy.[12]

There were exceptions to this rule, of course. Some jobbers developed reputations in highly-specialized lines and expanded rapidly to develop factory organization. Waterlows were a notable example. The founder, a descendant of Huguenot silk weavers, founded the business in the early nineteenth century in Birchin Lane in the City. This was a good site because commercial work was the basis of the firm's growth. A factory at Finsbury was already 'assuming enormous proportions' by 1850. By 1925 the firm had several large factories in the Finsbury area for its specialities, including banknotes and bankers' cheques. But already by that time it had devolved railway-ticket printing to a works at Bow and other work (including envelopes, lithographic posters and some banknote manufacture) to large single-floor factories at Dunstable and Watford.[13] Such a pattern of expansion was not possible for the smaller firm which characterized the industry. The small-master system had in fact the same effect in printing as in clothing: it tended to tie the industry as a whole more closely to its traditional sites.

In book printing, however, the equilibrium was rudely upset after 1850. Even before then there had been portents of what was to come. Clowes in 1843 had 24 steam-driven presses and complete vertical integration of production;[14] but they were the exception. Machinery invaded book production rapidly between 1850 and 1900. By then some parts of book work, for instance process blocks, had to be produced by machinery because such a strong impression was needed. The big steam-driven presses brought problems. When Clowes put the first in at their works in Charing Cross, the Duke of Northumberland, their neighbour, objected; Clowes had to move to Southwark. Unwins suffered constant complaints about their machinery and also had to move. The changeover to electricity about the beginning of this century brought relief, but by then many firms had migrated from central London.[15]

Pressure of space was not the only factor. Printing is a classic example of a trade which developed in a traditional centre and there gathered to itself a select, self-perpetuating group of skilled workers, which then itself became a critical factor of location. Printers were, in the words of one of them, 'above the ordinary standard of work-men'.[16] Readers were an educated group of men who would not be readily found anywhere outside a traditional centre of the trade; the compositors also had highly-developed special skills; the machinists needed a certain mechanical ability.[17] Further, the army of labourers and warehousemen was most easily supplied by London's reserve pool of labour. Labour supplies, therefore, tended to keep the industry tied to London up to 1850. In the later nineteenth century, however, the high cost of London labour began to weigh more and more heavily on the publishers. London rates were higher, and the tightly-organized compositors' and bookbinders' unions fought harder than their provincial brethren, in the 90's still often non-union-men. In book work about 1890 the average London weekly wage was 36s. to 38s. compared with 30s. in Edinburgh or Bristol, 27s. in Perth, 25s. to 26s. in Aylesbury or Ipswich, and about 20s. in some Irish towns.[18]

The provincial work, save in Oxford and Cambridge, was said at that time to be poorer in quality. But this disadvantage was being steadily overcome by the application of machinery to processes traditionally thought the province of skilled labour. A witness in the 90's was asked:

> But the trade has undergone great changes, has it not, in recent years through improved machinery?
> Yes, the tendency has been to divide it into departments far more than it used to be formerly. Apprentices are not taught now the whole trade as they used to be taught. They are only taught one portion of it.[19]

The pioneers in provincial work were Richard Clay, who had been printing successfully since 1820 in Suffolk, at Bungay. But it was only after 1850 that London publishers began to use provincial presses on a large scale. Many went to Watson and Hazell, periodical printers who had set up a book-printing branch at Aylesbury in 1867. Unwins sent their printing to Chilworth, Surrey, in 1871;

Clowes developed book printing at Beccles after 1873; the White-friars Press went to Tonbridge.[20] By the 90's a great many London printers were complaining of the competition of low-paid foreign labour. There was foreign competition also in a stricter sense, for at the turn of this century work was being put out to Holland and in lithography German competition was felt.[21] By 1930 the *New Survey of London Life and Labour* found that the trade was being rapidly enticed out of central London by lower wages and more space. Only newspaper and rapid commercial printing must remain.[22]

2. *Newspaper and periodical printing.* Newspaper printing evolved in London during the late sixteenth and early seventeenth centuries. Then, as now, the critical factor of news supply drew the industry to the capital. News came

> from sources that were almost identical with those of our own day: the republishing of foreign news items from printed papers, the official announcements, the private correspondents and contacts and the agency reports.[23]

All these were centralized in London, and remained so. In the eighteenth century London periodical publishing depended on the thrice-weekly posts from the provinces and abroad, which were important in the development of this branch of publishing.[24]

At the time of Waterloo the modern newspaper existed in embryo form in England, but there was no newspaper publishing and printing industry in the modern sense. Cobbett observed in 1802 that the *Morning Post*, then established thirty years and one of the best-known London dailies, sold only 1250 copies a day.[25] In 1817 *The Times* sold 6000 a day.[26] By 1900, however, a great indus-trial revolution had come over the trade. It was technical in nature, but it depended primarily upon the enormous potential increase in circulations made possible by the spread of popular education and by the repeal of the so-called 'taxes on knowledge'. Of these the most important was the newspaper stamp duty, repeal of which in 1855 made possible the penny press. The tax on advertisements was repealed in 1853, but its full effects were only to be seen after the rise in the 80's and 90's of the new popular journalism, founded on advertising revenue. The paper tax was repealed in 1861.

Two technical changes were necessary for newspapers to take advantage of the vast market thus created. First, newspapers had to be printed more quickly, and, secondly, they must be distributed at top speed.

The advances in printing technique came mainly from *The Times*, which had been installed since its foundation in 1784 in Printing House Square. In 1814 it introduced the Koenig cylinder press, one of the first steam-driven machines in London: it printed 1100 sheets an hour, four times as fast as the old hand presses, and it saved a great deal in compositors' wages, because single pages no longer needed to be duplicated. One commentator has called the invention of the machine 'an event of importance second only to that of the invention of printing itself'.[27] By 1825 improved versions of the Koenig machine had been developed, and other newspapers were following where *The Times* had led. Meanwhile *The Times* itself went further ahead, with a series that started with a four-feed press in 1827 and ended with a giant eight-feed rotary in 1848. This was the first true rotary machine which printed mangle-fashion. It printed 9600 copies an hour, nearly nine times as many as the Koenig machine of 1814. Such a machine was both necessary and profitable for *The Times*, whose circulation had risen from 6000 in 1817 to 38,000 in 1850. The repeal of the so-called 'taxes on knowledge' let loose a great circulation race which brought the *Daily Telegraph* (founded only in 1855) ahead of *The Times* in 1867 with 200,000, and made time an even more critical factor of production than before. *The Times* developed the improved rotary press in 1868-9; it printed from a continuous roll and cut printing time by half. But rotaries and improved rotaries merely upset the balance of production: the type could not now be set up quickly enough for the printers, a problem solved satisfactorily by the invention of the linotype machine in the late 80's. Other systems of machine setting arrived almost simultaneously. As a result, by the early 90's important news might be retailed in print ten minutes after it had happened.[28]

During the period 1820-80 other ancillary developments of great importance speeded and eased the art of newspaper printing: the centralized manufacture of printing ink, the rapid progress in type-founding, and especially the cheapening of paper through the introduction of woodpulp, beginning in 1850.[29]

The advances in distribution were as revolutionary. Until 1840 the post was virtually the only form of distribution outside London, and the number of papers sent by this means increased enormously in the late eighteenth and early nineteenth centuries, from an average of 3160 a day in 1764 to 41,400 in 1830. But as the mail coaches went quite early at night the news started from London already twelve hours old. After 1840 the Post Office found it possible to keep a share of the distribution of weekly periodicals, by offering special rates. But otherwise country-wide distribution depended henceforth on the railways. By 1847 W. H. Smith & Sons were already using nine special engines for their special newspaper trains; in 1848 their first London–Glasgow special made the journey in 10$\frac{1}{2}$ hours. In 1854 *The Times* gave them first priority of supply. *The Times*, however, further developed its own newspaper trains, which allowed it to arrive in the provinces three hours before its London rivals and compete on equal terms with the English provincial press. This system did not, however, last long.[30]

Rapid distribution chiefly enabled London national papers to compete successfully with provincial rivals. Other technical developments, however, restored the balance. Chief of these were the electric telegraph, cable and finally trunk telephone, which broke London's effective monopoly of news supply.

After 1890, however, a second revolution took place in newspaper publishing, partly conceptual and partly technical in nature. This was the advent of the new journalism, foreshadowed in the 80's by the weekly popular papers, *Tit-Bits* (1881, founded by George Newnes) and *Answers* (1888, founded by Alfred Harmsworth). The first truly modern popular paper was Harmsworth's *Daily Mail*, founded in 1896 and selling at $\frac{1}{2}d$. From the start the *Daily Mail* achieved unprecedented circulation levels. It sold an average of 202,000 copies in its first year and 989,000 by 1900.[31] This meant that the scale of production and the capital involved were greatly increased. Harmsworth paid £25,000 to launch the *Evening News*, £13,000 for the *Daily Mail*.[32] Naturally the *Daily Mail* was from the first a national daily, printed from London. A determined effort was made to reach the farthest parts of England by special deliveries, sometimes at uneconomic costs for a short period: at one time it was estimated that distribution in one area of south-west England cost 4d. a copy, though sales soon rose and made the venture pay[33].

In reaching this national market the London dailies had a clear advantage over their evening counterparts, which was summarized in 1949 by a Royal Commission:

> A morning paper can use the night, when the demand for news is silenced, to travel to distant markets. An evening paper has to meet a demand for fresh news hour by hour and indeed— since many are read primarily for their racing results—race by race: it cannot therefore ordinarily be sold much beyond an hour's journey by rail from its place of origin.[34]

The new journalism, then, continued like the old to rely upon the newspaper trains, which have now come to be operated by the Newspaper Proprietors' Association. The printing times of the London dailies were rigidly governed by the departure times of these trains. By 1930 at Euston alone there was every night a 7.30 p.m. to north Scotland, an 8.45 p.m. Irish Mail, an 11 p.m. to northern England, a 12.30 a.m. to Liverpool and Manchester, a 2.30 a.m. to Birmingham and a 2.35 a.m. to Liverpool.[35]

However, it was the *Daily Mail* which pioneered, only a few years after its foundation, the process of simultaneous publication in London and Manchester, using private-wire transmission of chief news items.[36] Most of the *Mail*'s competitors emulated it in the 20's and 30's. By 1948 all the nationals except *The Times*, the *Mirror* and the *Worker* printed in Manchester, and the *Express* and the *Mail* also in Scotland.[37]

With the evening papers, as the quotation above indicates, it has been a different matter. They have survived the competition of London, though often their management has been taken over by chains centred there. In 1948 provincial morning papers had a combined circulation of only 2·7 million as compared with the 15·6 million of the London dailies. In evening papers the provinces had, however, 6·8 million against London's 3·5 million.[38] For evening papers, then, provincial publishing survives as it does not in daily-paper production. The mass-circulation daily newspapers themselves, however, have found it profitable to devolve the printing process to provincial centres.

The economics of location for newspaper publishing may therefore be regarded as governed in this century by two contradictory principles. One is the necessity for rapid contact with the market; the other, economies of scale. In daily-newspaper production the former factor is minimized by the possibility of night distribution, and the economies of large-scale production are dominant. In 1951 the average establishment in newspaper and periodical printing in the United Kingdom had 130 workers, and 84 per cent of all workers in the trade were in establishments of more than 100 workers.[39] This is unusual for a central London manufacturing industry, and also unusual is the fact that the industry makes large demands on raw materials and power. The annual consumption of newsprint by the industry in the entire country in the 30's was of the order of 1,270,000 tons.[40] In 1930 the horse-power per operative in the industry was 1·94, more than double that for other forms of printing.[41] Despite these facts, the industry remains tied to central London, and an historian of printing in London recently concluded:

> The day has not yet come when the last branch of the printing trade to be substantially represented in the capital can plan to depart, nor in our day will newspaper printing in London become a legend; whereas the London book printing houses are now forgotten sites and the job printers require the incentive of freeholds or of firm contracts.[42]

In evening-paper production, however, the necessity of immediate touch with the market has kept the industry much smaller in scale, and dispersed in location.

In periodical printing, where the timetable is naturally more leisurely than that of the newspaper, the twentieth century has seen a marked division between the publishing process and the printing process. Printing has often found it economically possible to hive off, if not to the provinces then to the suburbs. The stipulation that *Hansard* be printed in Greater London had already been waived by 1900, and it was being found possible to print weekly journals in the provinces; all you needed in London was a counter.[43] In 1901 an observer commented:

> ... despite these possibilities of inconvenience, and these dire risks of a delay that cannot but spell disaster, not only leisurely book production, but the more rapid and irritating printing of

periodicals, is being forced by financial necessities beyond the zone of Metropolitan extravagance.[44]

Although this tendency proceeded apace in this century, it left the publishing process unaffected, for central London remained the home of most sorts of specialized intelligence. So that the Royal Commission in 1949 could say:

> The publication of periodicals is centralised in London to a greater degree even than that of newspapers. With the exception of a group of magazines published in Glasgow, Dundee, and Manchester, all the more widely circulated periodicals and magazines of general interest originate in London; so also do most of the trade and technical publications and about four-fifths of the political periodicals.[45]

For the printing industry the essential factor of location is that summed up by a writer on printing trades in the City of New York: 'the importance of the elements of time and personal contact'.[46] These elements have already been found to be of the greatest importance to other old-established London trades, in particular clothing. In all these trades, however, the importance of the factor has been somewhat eroded away in the present century by improved communications and by the growth of factory production. It continues to tie to central locations those branches of industry dependent upon novelty as a basic principle of sale: women's outerwear and daily-newspaper printing. Where the response to the demands of the market is more predictable or less immediate, then the industry has deserted its traditional sites, particularly where the development of factory production has increased demands on space and weakened the hold of traditional labour pools.

1 G. E. Arkell in C. Booth (ed.), *Life and Labour of the People in London* (1892–7), VI, 190.
2 Ibid., 229.
3 *New Survey of London Life and Labour* (1930–5), V, 268.
4 This paragraph is based on E. Howe and H. E. Waite, *The London Society of Compositors: A Centenary History* (1948), 1–4; H. R. Plomer, *A Short History of English Printing, 1476–1900* (1915), 27, 31–6; M. Plant, *The English Book Trade* (1939), 80–2, 165–6.

5 R. A. A. Leigh, *The Story of a Printing House* (1912), 2–8.
6 F. C. R. and H. G. Harrison, *The House of Harrison* (1914), 1, 4, 6–10, 51–6.
7 W. T. Berry in C. Singer and others (ed.), *A History of Technology*, V (Oxford 1958), 709–11.
8 E. Howe and H. E. Waite, op. cit., 147–8.
9 G. E. Arkell, op. cit., 233; H. L. Williams, *The Worker's Industrial Index to London* (1881), 12.
10 *Census of Production 1951*, vol. 10. For the U.K. it was 32·3.
11 Dr E. Smith, *Sanitary Circumstances of Printers in London:* Appendix to *Sixth Report of the Medical Officer of the Privy Council*, 390–1, *P.P.* 1864, XXVIII.
12 *R. C. Labour Minutes, Group C*, Q. 22955, *P.P.* 1893–4, XXXIV.
13 J. Boon, *Under Six Reigns* (1925), 2–6, 29–40.
14 G. Dodd, *Days at the Factories* (1843), 327, 347.
15 M. Plant, op. cit., 278–9, 289.
16 R. C. Labour, op. cit., Q. 22687.
17 Dr E. Smith, op. cit., 387, 390, 404–5.
18 G. E. Arkell, op. cit., 196.
19 R. C. Labour, op. cit., Q. 22811.
20 P. M. Handover, *Printing in London from 1476 to Modern Times* (1960), 211; P. W. Wilson in C. F. G. Masterman (ed.), *The Heart of the Empire* (1901), 213.
21 Ibid., 212; R. C. Labour, op. cit., Q. 22710.
22 New Survey, op. cit., V, 267.
23 P. M. Handover, op. cit., 106.
24 Ibid., 125.
25 H. Tracey (ed.), *The British Press* (1929), 14.
26 E. Howe, *Newspaper Printing in the Nineteenth Century* (1943), 9.
27 J. Southward, *Progress in Printing and the Graphic Arts during the Victorian Era* (1897), 33.
28 *The History of The Times*, I, 1785–1841 (1935), 3–5; P. M. Handover, op. cit., 83–4, for the origin of Printing House Square; E. Howe and H. E. Waite, op. cit., 151–4; E. Howe, op. cit., 1–19, 23–8, 41–2; G. E. Arkell, op. cit., 197.
29 H. Tracey, op. cit., 16.
30 Paragraph based on *The Times*, Empire Press Number (31 May 1930), xiii–xv.
31 P. E. P., *Report on the British Press* (1938), 93–4.
32 M. Grünbeck, *Die Presse Grossbritanniens* (Leipzig 1936), I, 31.
33 F. A. McKenzie, *The Mystery of the Daily Mail* (1921), 115.
34 *R. C. Press, Report*, 10, *P.P.* 1948–9, XX.
35 *Times*, Empire Press Number, op. cit., xv.
36 H. Tracey, op. cit., 29; F. A. Mackenzie, op. cit., 101.
37 R. C. Press, op. cit., 8.
38 Ibid., 12–13.
39 *Census of Production 1951*, vol. 10.
40 Calculation from P. E. P., op. cit., 4–5.

41 *Census of Production 1930*, part III, 441:

42 P. M. Handover, op. cit., 170.

43 P. W. Wilson, op. cit., 213.

44 Ibid., 214.

45 R. C. Press, op. cit., 14.

46 A. F. Hinrichs, *The Printing Industry in New York and its Environs*. (Plan of New York and its Environs. Economic Series Monographs, 6, New York 1924), 38–9.

7

THE OLDER INDUSTRIES: CONCLUSIONS

BEFORE reaching general conclusions about the location patterns of
the older trades, it is necessary to reiterate a distinction between
what the Barlow Commission called the service industries, and what
it called the basics. This distinction is well drawn by Aves in his
conclusions on London industry in the final volume of the Booth
Survey:

> Certain of its operations in distribution and in trading; all
> forms of service rendered to persons or groups of persons; all
> labour expended on permanent fixtures, such as buildings or
> streets, must, it is true, be necessarily carried on in its midst.[1]

These are the trades

> when the convenience of meeting a local demand by local
> sources of supply is exceptionally great, as in baking, brewing,
> and the printing of newspapers.[2]

In so far as these are truly local services—as Aves' examples only
partially are—they require no complex analysis of location. But,
Aves continued:

> . . . in a few cases only does the locality of a demand
> determine also the locality of an industry, and the great bulk of
> the trades of London remain liable to displacement.[3]

It is with this class of long-established industries that this
chapter is concerned; the conclusions reached about them are as
follows:

Materials

Materials are usually light and small in bulk; they are in fact often already semi-processed; and the cost of transporting them is negligible in relation to total cost of production, so that no one location has on this basis any advantage over another. Such are the clothing, shoemaking and precious-metals trades. In addition some industries, such as piano manufacture, use diverse raw materials which must be assembled from various sources. Here London has an advantage as the greatest national focus of both internal and external lines of trade. In the few cases where the material is bulky or heavy, which occur as a rule in the earlier stages of production, London profits from her splendid water-transport facilities. The trade of the port of London is chiefly a destination trade, for consumption in or near London.[4] The industries which depend on bulky imported raw materials are commonly found near the docks.[5] In London they include sugar refining, leather tanning and the manufacture of furniture. The port industries are one great group of London trades. Commonly they process their imported raw materials into a form ready for use by other industries—sugar refining serves confectionery, and the old Bermondsey tanning yards served the shoemaking industry.

Fuel and power

The older type of London industry is not dependent upon coal for fuel, and rarely for power. In the nineteenth century it commonly used hand- or foot-driven machinery, or no machinery at all, while its well-developed gas industry, fed by coal brought by water from the Tyne or by rail from the Midlands, provided the heat for the tailor's pressing-iron or the baker's oven. Because it lacked coal London lacked the characteristic nineteenth-century coalfield industries, such as iron and steel manufacture or heavy engineering, which are perhaps most commonly thought typical of the Industrial Revolution. But other great nineteenth-century concentrations of population, like Hull or Liverpool, also lacked such industries. Their industry conformed to a different pattern, but one equally typical in its way: that of the great port, the source of imported raw material.[6] London was however more than just this.

The market

In one form or another, nearness to the market has been the original locating factor for most of the older London trades. But London's role as market is a complex one. If it were not, we might well conclude that the great bulk of London industry consisted of local services, and that the capital was a self-contained economic unit, engaged in supplying its own needs. This is however far from the case, for London's market function has at least three aspects.

First, ever since its foundation London has been the largest single centre of population in the country. Admittedly, the Industrial Revolution created great industrial conurbations in midland and northern England. But no rival can approach London in size and degree of population concentration. For consumer goods—a category which includes the largest of the old-established trades—London therefore provides the greatest single market in the country. Because of the concentration of national routes upon the capital, it is also in an exceptionally easy position to reach provincial markets.

But, secondly, the consumption of London relative to the rest of the country is undoubtedly much higher than a mere count of heads would indicate. This arises from the exceptional concentration in the capital of the market for luxury and semi-luxury goods, which in turn has two causes. On the one hand, London contains an exceptional proportion of very rich individuals and institutions. On the other hand, it is the great central service centre and retail emporium of the country. It bears the same relation to the provinces, especially to those parts south of the latitude of Birmingham, that a rural market town bears to its surrounding villages. These causes arise in their turn from London's historical development as capital city, first of a nation, then of a united kingdom, lastly of a great commercial empire. Already by the time of Bede it had one historic function as 'the mart of many nations resorting to it by sea and land'.[7] The second, the government function, came much later. In the early Middle Ages the maintenance of order throughout the kingdom required a decentralized or a mobile government. After the Norman Conquest the government of England became centralized, but still mobile: permanence was achieved in stages from the reign of Henry II onwards. First the Exchequer, then the Treasury, later still the Common and King's Benches, finally

Parliament, settled in London. The process was more or less achieved by the end of the fourteenth century.[8] It was a natural one, for the economic centre of medieval England, both internally in terms of agricultural and industrial wealth and externally in terms of European trade, was southern England; and of that half of the country London was the natural centre.

In the centuries following 1400, then, the establishment of government in London inevitably led to its development as a centre of conspicuous consumption. An extravagant Court made its demands felt there. The government spent its revenues there. The judicial arm of the government produced an important professional group of lawyers there, to add to the existing professional group of Civil Servants, of whom Chaucer was one. Lastly, in the sixteenth century, the landed gentry became town-dwellers. They made London's Inns of Court their place of education, and afterwards found in the capital a land market (the Crown Lands sales), a money market and a marriage market. The result, in Elizabeth's time, was the first great growth of the luxury trades, the services, building, entertainment. And at this time also came the fundamental division of London into a poor producing east and a rich consuming west, 'a district of wealth and leisure stretching towards Westminster and the Court',[9] as it was in the later sixteenth century. This age saw also the opening up of the new continents, which was to produce two centuries later a great new class grown rich in trade to further augment the luxury market of the capital.[10]

In these centuries there was but one sort of industry: handicraft industry. Since its methods of production were necessarily expensive, the bulk of its production went to a luxury market that had come to be located disproportionately in London. In the final stages of such production the bespoke system naturally prevailed, as in tailoring, shoemaking, furniture and precious metals. Consequently the industry must be found within immediate personal reach of its consuming market: this was especially so before 1750 because of the inadequacy of transport and communication. Although then these trades were theoretically, in Aves' words, 'liable to displacement', they were until recent times in the nature of service industries. But a service trade too may export its products: the luxury market of the provinces came to London to get its best clothes and shoes and furniture made. This then is the origin of a second great group of traditional London trades, which may be called the West End craft industries.

There was however yet a third aspect to London as a market. After the sacking of Antwerp by the Duke of Parma in 1585, and after a brief period in which Amsterdam vied for the title, London became at least until the first world war the financial centre of the world. Most of the speculative money which came to London undoubtedly arose from foreign trade and arrived in the City as the centre of that trade. Here it readily united with a tradition of production even older than that of the West End trades—that of the City craft industries—to conceive a new system of production, in which a middleman ordered goods as the agent of a final consumer, whose identity was at the time of ordering uncertain. Capital was used therefore to buy goods in advance of final demand, and in the speculation of their resale at profit. The precise date of origin of this system is obscure. Ben Jonson's reference to 'a *Hounds-ditch* man, sir. One of the deuil's neere kinsmen, a broker' indicates that speculative capital was doing its work in the City by 1598 in the second-hand-clothing trade, and by 1800 the wholesale system seems to have been firmly established in certain trades within particular localities at the edge of the City: clothing, the oldest, in Whitechapel; boots and shoes and furniture in Finsbury and Shoreditch. Both systems, the West End trade for the retail bespoke market, the City trade for the wholesale ready-made market, were in their very different ways market-orientated; both engaged in the final assembly of valuable, light, often semi-processed materials into consumer goods.

Labour

The industries originally established because of these factors have in many cases been powerfully aided by London's labour supplies. The central feature of the London labour market is its size: London's enormous population makes it certain that, for most purposes, 'One has usually but to hold up the finger to secure whatever men are needed'.[11] But the labour market, like the consumers' market, has different aspects.

First, there are in London exceptional concentrations of labour skilled in certain narrow directions. These concentrations have been of greatest importance in the West End luxury trades: they have in most cases been originally called forth by the existence and the demands of the local market and have then perpetuated themselves near to it. But in certain cases the existence of the labour seems virtually to have called forth the demand, as in the case of the trades created by skilled refugees from Europe: Spitalfields silk or Hatton Garden jewellery. This is the explanation of the fact that some trades, though catering for a luxury market, have traditionally been located not immediately adjacent to that market; they have instead remained in those areas close to the point of arrival of the immigrants, at the edge of the City: Clerkenwell, Hatton Garden, Spitalfields, Whitechapel.

The second great element in the London labour market is usually termed the unskilled-labour pool. This is perhaps a misleading term: even the immigrant greener of the 80's had to make considerable material sacrifice to learn his highly specialized chosen skill in the tailoring or bootmaking trades. Rather is it true to say that London has of all centres the greatest pool of adaptable labour, unskilled but ready to acquire fairly-elementary skills, especially since 1850 in the handling of a simple machine. This labour pool has contained two main elements. First is the army of female labour, a result of the lack in London of a single great female-employing manufacturing trade such as cotton in Lancashire. This army attracts parasitic trades to the areas of heavy male employment in London, the dock areas in particular. The second element is the immigrants. These have been in one form or another a permanent and apparently essential part of London industrial life since we have records. The Irish in the eighteenth century; the Russian and Polish Jews of the 1880's; the West Indian, Pakistani and Cypriot immigrants of our own day: all have provoked resentment and even physical violence in the areas where they first settled, all have provided for a time a vital service in performing grades of work which native labour was reluctant to undertake; all, if historical experience is a guide, have within a relatively short time been integrated successfully into the native social and economic systems, leaving new immigrant groups to fill the gap. The immigrants from the provinces of England were less easily distinguished, and so are less completely documented. But they came in enormous numbers, as the birthplace tables of the nineteenth-century Censuses show: and undoubtedly they mainly went to swell the pool of unskilled labour.

External economies

General—and more importantly—specific external economies have been of the greatest importance in the location of London's traditional trades. This is so because both the retail bespoke and the wholesale ready-made systems of production in London, producing articles for consumption, require not only small bulk of material but also little capital equipment for their processing; and thereby encourage the small-master or the home systems of production, which may commonly unite in the home workshop, as with the Hackney shoemaker, the Clerkenwell jeweller or the Soho tailor. This system is in most cases accompanied by at least some division of labour and consequent vertical disintegration of production, whereby separate processes of production are given to separate individual workers or to separate small masters in their own places of work. Of great importance in this system are the ancillary works for the supply or servicing of main or accessory materials or equipment—sewing-machine depots, timber yards, sawmills, grindery shops or cabinet-makers' tool shops. Given this form of organization, the principle of linkage inevitably concentrates the small individual units of production into a restricted quarter which thereafter no one unit may with impunity leave. The attraction of the quarter is further strengthened by the exceptional importance for many of these trades of taste, fashion, novelty and season; which necessitates the quick production of small orders, and ensures that every man in the trade must have intelligence of its latest, perhaps idiosyncratic, trends. All those qualities enumerated in Marshall's famous passage on external economies therefore apply to the traditional trades of the London quarters in the highest degree. Failing then a change to a system of production in large factories, which by their nature are more independent in their location decisions than is the small unit, the traditional quarter should continue to dominate the location of many London trades, despite all the disadvantages of overcrowded workshops which are alike unhealthy for the employed and uneconcmic for the employer—in high rates and rents, in ill-planned working conditions, and in congested transport facilities for materials and for finished product. The principle of location of many traditional London consumer-goods trades, then, as the Booth Survey declared in the 90's, is *'J'y suis, j'y reste'*.[12]

1　E. Aves in C. Booth (ed.), *Life and Labour of the People in London*, IX, 178–9.
2　Ibid., 186.
3　Ibid., 179.
4　*Report R. C. Administration of the Port of London*, 21, *P.P.* 1902, XLIII.
5　J. H. Bird, *Geography of the Port of London* (1957), Chapter VII.
6　Wilfred Smith (ed.), *A Scientific Study of Merseyside* (British Association, Liverpool 1953), 171.
7　*Bede's Ecclesiastical History of the English Nation* (Everyman edition 1910), 68.
8　T. F. Tout, 'The Beginnings of a Modern Capital: London and Westminster in the fourteenth century', *Proceedings of the British Academy*, 10 (1921–3), 487–511.
9　M. D. George, *London Life in the XVIIIth Century* (1925), 63.
10　F. J. Fisher, 'The Development of London as a centre of Conspicuous Consumption in the Sixteenth and Seventeenth Centuries', *Transactions of the Royal Historical Society*, 4th series, XXX (1948), 37–50.
11　E. Aves, op. cit, 181.
12　Ibid., 186.

8

THE NEW INDUSTRIAL AREAS

THE rest of this book is about the newer industries, which were most important in the rapid industrialization of parts of outer London between 1918 and 1939. It has already been seen that some of the older trades discussed in Chapters 4–7 expanded greatly in the interwar years, and migrated to the Outer Ring. Furniture, clocks and precision instruments are examples. But most of the industrial growth of outer London during this period was due to industries which existed only on a very small scale, or not at all, in 1861. Examples of these industries are general engineering, electrical engineering and vehicle manufacture, each of which is discussed in detail in Chapters 9–11. The present chapter is intended to serve as an introduction to the newer industries. It chronicles historically the physical development of the most important of the new industrial areas of London. These areas, as already shown in Chapter 3, were predominantly in the county of Middlesex. The account given here draws on two detailed investigations of industrial development in Middlesex, one published (but long out of print), the other unpublished.

In 1951 no less than 26·2 per cent of the total manufacturing workers of London were in the county of Middlesex, and of these 5·3 per cent were found in the Lea Valley manufacturing zone and 17·3 per cent in the West Middlesex manufacturing zone. The growth of these great manufacturing areas was described by a contemporary witness, D. H. Smith, in 1933. At that date Smith estimated the total employment in manufacturing (excluding building) in Middlesex at 117,400.[1]

It is clear from Table 12 that the two great manufacturing zones had already evolved in 1933, though the West Middlesex zone at least was still in process of rapid development. Smith traced the growth of both areas in great detail from the year 1900.

TABLE 12

MANUFACTURING EMPLOYMENT IN MIDDLESEX, 1933
(Source: D. H. Smith)

Lea Valley industrial zone	*37700*
North Middlesex residential zone	*3100*
West Middlesex industrial zone:	*75000*
Hendon–Edgware	13500
Wembley–Greenford–Park Royal–Willesden	28800
Acton (The Vale)	7500
Southall–Hayes	14100
Brentford–Chiswick–Heston–Isleworth	11100
Uxbridge–Yiewsley	*1600*
Total	117400[1]

The Lea Valley zone

By this Smith meant the west side of the lower Lea Valley below Enfield. In 1900 this zone had already over 20 firms; by 1933 the figure was over 120. Of the additional 100 firms, only 40 were new. Fifty-six had moved from other parts of Greater London. Twenty-three of these did not reveal precisely where they had come from. Of the remaining 33, 23 had come from what has been called in this book the Victorian manufacturing belt, as defined narrowly from the 1861 Census; and no less than 31 from the enlarged Victorian manufacturing belt as defined on the basis of the 1951 Census statistics. Only four firms had moved from outside London altogether. Smith's findings therefore powerfully confirm the view, already proposed tentatively in Chapter 3 of this book, that the Lea Valley represented the natural line of expansion for firms in the Victorian manufacturing belt of London.

Smith gave an analysis of employment for 35,000 workers in the Lea Valley zone. In Table 13 this has been compared with the structure of employment in manufacturing for Greater London as shown in the industrial tables of the 1931 Census, so as to obtain a Local Location Quotient for the Lea Valley zone at this date. Both older and newer industries were thus well represented. Though Smith gave no detailed analysis, it seems at least probable that the older industries represented firms which had moved out of congested parts of inner London, and the newer industries mainly represented the completely new firms.

The most important point about the Lea Valley zone, however, is that both older and new industries seem to have been influenced by similar factors of location. In general transport costs were not important. Except for furniture, the Lea Valley industries used only small amounts of material, easily obtained by rail or road. Typical materials were copper rods, sheet metal and wire, obtained by road from the Midlands. The finished products also were usually small

TABLE 13

LEA VALLEY: LEADING MANUFACTURING INDUSTRIES, 1933

(Source: D. H. Smith; Census, 1931)

	Numbers	Percentage total manufacturing employment	Local Location Quotient
Electrical engineering	6750	19·3	2·6
Clothing (excluding footwear)	4475	12·8	0·7
Furniture	3690	10·6	2·1
Stationery	2750	7·9	2·8
General engineering	2720	7·8	1·2
Footwear	1950	5·6	2·8
Vehicles	1450	4·2	0·8[2]

and easily transported—for instance motor parts, accumulators, stationery, pencils, toys. But ready access to market was extremely important, even though it could not be easily analysed in cost terms. The market for the Lea Valley industries might mean three things: the London wholesale and retail market; the docks, for the export trade; and the London rail termini and road exits, for home distribution. For all these the area was well situated. Second in importance to market access was labour supply. The area had a large population of skilled, semi-skilled and unskilled workers, as a result of the great wave of cheap house building between 1880 and 1900, which had attracted a working-class population to Tottenham and Edmonton. The third important factor was space and cheap land. In the early days of industrial development, up to 1914, land was relatively cheap and rateable values low in Tottenham and Edmonton. By the late 20's, ironically, congestion and high land values were the rule, but by then the great migration had occurred. All the firms that had moved to the Lea Valley from other parts of London quoted cheap land as a factor; over half of them gave it as the primary one. It was by far the commonest factor quoted among *all* firms analysed, as Table 14 shows.

TABLE 14

LEA VALLEY: PRIMARY FACTORS IN LOCATION, UP TO 1933

(Source: D. H. Smith)

		Numbers	Percentage of total
1	Space: more needed for extension	29 }41	22 }31
	Cheaper land, rent, rates	12	9
2	Existing buildings	15	11
3	London market	11	8
4	Transport facilities	16	12
5	Cheap labour	11	8
6	Owner lived near factory	16	12
7	Other reasons, or unknown	21	16
		131	100[2]

The factors governing the location of the industries of the Lea Valley in 1933, therefore, were in no way different from those governing the location of industries in the inner East End in 1890, except that space had perhaps become more important with the development of factory production in some of the older industries. But even here it must be recalled that the small furniture work-shops of the Curtain Road area in 1890 had in their turn been driven out of the City not many decades previously by lack of space and rising land values. The process has been continuous.

Smith concluded:

Most of the industries situated in this area supply the needs of a large town population; they are not necessarily luxury industries, which is the case with so many industries in the western sector of Greater London. Many of them cater for a section of workers with a low standard of living.[3]

This conclusion on the Lea Valley industries would have applied equally well to the traditional East End trades of 1890. By 1930, however, the low standard of living was higher, and the range of products it demanded was consequently greater.

In the later 1930's the industrial development of the Lea Valley proceeded along the same lines, though more rapidly. In the years 1935–8 inclusive, the Board of Trade Surveys of Industrial Development show that 68 new factories were opened in the area, almost exactly three times the number opened in the period 1928–31 inclusive. Of these 32 were completely new and 36 were transfers. No less than 22 of the transfers were from the inner East End (including Finsbury); 12 were from other parts of Greater London; and only two were from outside London altogether. Of the 22 firms arriving from the inner East End, 18 were in older industries, including 12 in furniture and associated wood products.

The West Middlesex industrial zone: geographical pattern

When Smith analysed the West Middlesex industrial zone in 1933 some parts of it were still under development, and others were as yet hardly developed. The area was analysed again in great detail in 1952 by B. A. Bates.[4] By this time development was virtually complete and there was little room for further physical expansion save on the extreme western margin of the county. The analysis given here of the development of this zone is based mainly on these two important accounts.

Even in 1933 this was a much larger industrial zone than the Lea Valley, both in geographical extent and in total activity; at that time it employed almost twice as many workers as the Lea Valley zone. It was also much more complex.

> The area is not homogeneous in its development . . . there is a tendency for zones of industrial growth to alternate with residential areas.[5]

This was the pattern which Bates found also, in 1952. Apart from ubiquitous local service centres, catering for the needs of the neighbourhood with industries such as baking, tailoring, shoe repairing, dry cleaning and electrical repairs, industry was sharply segregated:

> Industry in West London tends to occur in pockets of varying size and importance.[6]

At one extreme was the Park Royal industrial area, with 335 acres given over to industry in 1952; at the other, the Great West Road (New Brentford) with only 15·6 acres. Physically these concentrations were very varied: some spread in haphazard fashion along main roads, others had a degree of incipient planning along service or access roads. Bates distinguished 15 major concentrations of industry in west London in 1952. (One of these, North Hammersmith, was in the County of London.) Together they accounted for 107,470 workers, or just over two-fifths of all the manufacturing workers in the zone. In Table 15 they are set out in order of size.

TABLE 15

WEST LONDON: LEADING MANUFACTURING AREAS, 1952
(Source: B. A. Bates)

	No. of firms	Total employment
Park Royal	302	31680
Hayes	66	21140
Southall	21	7990
Acton, The Vale	29	7430
Colindale	45	5940
Staples Corner	82	5620
Willesden High Road	126	4040
Wembley: East Lane	10	3930
Wembley: Exhibition Grounds	81	3870
North Hammersmith	34	3740
Perivale	55	3490
Alperton, Ealing Road	51	3130
Mount Pleasant	71	2470
The Hyde	17	1980
Honeypot Lane	21	1020
Total	1011	107470
Total manufacturing workers in West London		249700[6]

These pockets may be grouped for convenience into wider industrial sub-zones, which together make up the West Middlesex industrial zone. Even by 1933, however, these sub-zones were virtually contiguous with one another. Today they form an almost continuous zone of manufacturing from Colindale and Hendon in the north, running south through Wembley and Willesden to Park Royal and Acton in the south-east, and thence in a broad belt westwards, with concentrations along the main traffic arteries: Western Avenue (Perivale–Greenford), the old G.W.R. main line (Southall–Hayes) and the Great West Road (Brentford).

Within West Middlesex four chief sub-zones can be distinguished. They were already apparent by 1933.

1. *Colindale–Hendon–Edgware Road*. Here the largest concentrations in 1933 were along the North Circular Road and in Cricklewood. The origin of development was the aircraft and munition factories at The Hyde, Colindale, which were transferred to private developers in 1920.

2. *The Wembley–Willesden–Park Royal–Perivale–Greenford triangle*. This was by far the most important single concentration, and has remained so. Indeed it is the greatest single concentration of manufacturing industry in southern England. Within the zone it is possible to distinguish germinal areas of pre-1914 development —for instance in Acton. Much of this consisted of small firms haphazardly located in the midst of residential property, often indeed in converted dwelling houses. Willesden was an exception. Here the pre-1914 development had included some large works, notably British Thomson-Houston and McVitie and Price. These were established on the northern border of what was to become the Park Royal industrial district. They were dependent on the excellent facilities for bulk handling of goods by rail (Willesden Junction) and even canal (the Grand Union). Between the wars other large plants were attracted to this area, including the Heinz food-processing plant which with 1500 workers was the largest factory in the Park Royal area in 1952. At that date Bates found that the average firm here had 387·0 workers, compared with 105·2 for the whole Park Royal area.

The real origin of development in Park Royal, however, was very different. It lay in the munitions factories established during the first world war by the government at Park Royal. After 1918 they lay derelict until they were bought in the 20's by a firm for scrap-metal sorting. Only after purchase did the company realize that there was a large unsatisfied demand from small manufacturing firms which could not raise enough capital to build a factory, but would offer good prices for ready-built factories. The company therefore began to build cheap 'all-purpose' factories in Park Royal, from 1929 onwards, and later to sell factories on credit with a 30 per cent cash deposit. They produced a new factory every ten to fourteen days, and soon had many more applicants than vacancies.

As a result, Park Royal has come to be dominated by the small plant. Bates concluded:

> Though Park Royal is the most important industrial area of London, it is not remarkable for the number of very large factories it contains.

Figure 21 shows the distribution of industry in Park Royal in 1952 according to Bates. At that date the area covered 355 acres, bounded on the north by the London Midland main line passing through Willesden Junction; on the west by the Guinness brewery and the Abbey Road industrial area; on the east by the Willesden Junction–Acton Central railway line; and on the south by Western Avenue (though the zone projects beyond Western Avenue on the south-west corner). Within this area were 305 firms, only five of which had more than 1000 workers in 1952. At that date the average Park Royal firm had 105·2 workers, but this figure was inflated by the few larger firms on the periphery of the estate, especially in the north. In the centre the average dropped as low as 49; here the most typical factory was the small general engineering plant. Throughout the estate the average general engineering plant was small; entry into the industry was easy, plant costs low, demand for skilled labour limited and market guaranteed in the form of orders from large concerns such as Fords. In vehicles the average size of plant was reduced by the large number of small repair shops. Only in food processing and electrical engineering did the big firm have an important place. For the whole Park Royal estate in 1952 the average number of workers per plant was 73·0 in general engineering, 122·8 in vehicles (183·3 excluding repair shops), 202·1 in food,

drink and tobacco, and 230·9 in electrical engineering. Bates concluded that the small workshop would continue to dominate Park
Royal, though the average size might increase slightly as the area
matured industrially. Park Royal may therefore be regarded as the
classic case of the continuing strength of the London small-work-
shop tradition in the mid-twentieth century.[7]

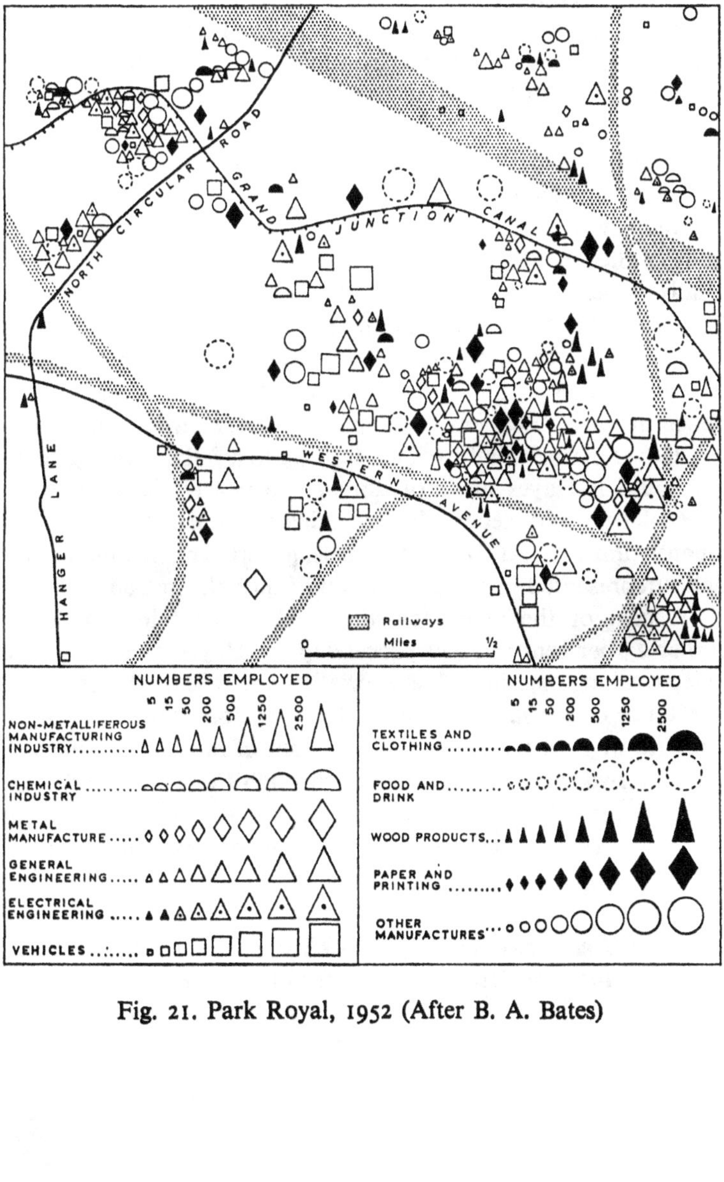

Fig. 21. Park Royal, 1952 (After B. A. Bates)

The Wembley Exhibition site is another example of an industrial area which originated in existing buildings. Here they were the structures erected for the British Empire Exhibitions of 1924 and 1925. Still in industrial use are two large palaces—one with $11\frac{1}{4}$ acres, another with 13 acres—and three smaller pavilions. General and electrical engineering together accounted for 42 per cent of employment in 1952. For industrial purposes the site has considerable disadvantages: access from outside is limited by railway tracks on three sides, while the internal road system was intended only for pedestrian use and is quite inadequate for the heavy goods traffic which has to use it today.

3. *Southall–Hayes*. Development in this area has followed a pattern very different from that in Park Royal. In both cases the large factory 'colonized' the area and initiated development. When Smith studied Southall–Hayes in 1933 it was dominated by exceptionally large factories, notably the Gramophone Company in Hayes and the Associated Equipment Company in Southall. The average firm in the area at that time appears to have been nearly twice as large as in the West Middlesex area as a whole. The difference lies in subsequent development. Bates showed that though Park Royal matured industrially, leading to a fall in average factory size, Southall–Hayes had not done so to nearly the same extent. The structure and geography of industry in the area were consequently unusual. At the 1951 Census, general engineering was very weakly represented in both Hayes and Southall; in Southall nearly 40 per cent of the manufacturing workers were in vehicles and another 25 per cent in food processing; in Hayes 51 per cent were in electrical engineering. This specialization reflects the continuing importance of the large factory, relying not on road transport but on the railway for materials and shipment of finished products. No major interwar arterial road passes through the area; the factories are distributed in a linear pattern along the main line of the old Great Western Railway, so as to give maximum space for sidings.

4. *The Great West Road (Chiswick–Staines)*. In this area there was a pre-1914 nucleus round Brentford Dock. Here the early industries depended upon water transport: timber, chemicals,

brewing, tug repairing and milling. Later the industrial base broadened and by 1952 engineering, both general and electrical, dominated the industrial structure.

The interwar industrial development depended upon the construction of the Great West Road in the early 20's. Some of the outermost, last-developed areas came to be dominated by a single large factory: Feltham by gyroscope manufacture; Staines by linoleum; Sunbury by thermostatic equipment. In 1952 these areas were still, in Bates' phrase, 'industrially immature'.

The West Middlesex industrial zone: industrial structure

The industrial structure of the West Middlesex industrial zone at the Census of 1951 has already been touched upon in the introduction to Chapter 4, where it was found that the older-established industries of London were in most cases very weakly established there. The area contained, in 1951, 17·3 per cent of the manufacturing workers of Greater London. But it contained only 9·1 per cent of the furniture workers; 6·0 per cent of the printers; and 2·8 per cent of the clothes-makers. In contrast many of the newer-established trades were very strongly represented in this zone. It contained in 1951 18·4 per cent of the engineering workers of London; 29·2 per cent of the electrical engineering workers; 29·2 per cent of vehicle-makers; and 27·8 per cent of workers in food processing.

This industrial structure was already fully evolved when Smith studied the area in 1933. Three industrial groups—vehicles, electrical engineering and foodstuffs—were then of outstanding importance, accounting for 58·8 per cent of total manufacturing employment in the area. Next came chemicals and after that general engineering. Within the area there were certain local concentrations. Thus electrical engineering was most strongly concentrated in the Southall–Hayes area; vehicle manufacture in the Vale, Acton; and chemical manufacture in the Great West Road belt. These concentrations arose largely from the fact that already by that time certain industries and industrial areas were dominated by single large factories, and this in turn was associated with the fact that 'the manufacture of proprietary articles is a dominating type of industry'. Many of these were what Smith called luxuries, though they might be given a different name today.

Generally speaking, the bulk of the industries are engaged in the manufacture of products which are either luxury products, e.g., gramophones, cars, perfumes, or products which are used for the manufacture of other luxury products, e.g., non-splinterable glass, chromium plating, tyres, etc.[8]

The domination of the West Middlesex industrial zone by the newer industries helps to explain the fact that, compared with the Lea Valley, a larger proportion of the plants established there by 1933 were not transfers from inner London, but completely new establishments. This was especially marked in Chiswick–Staines, where almost two-thirds were new.

TABLE 16

LEA VALLEY AND WEST MIDDLESEX: NEW FIRMS AND TRANSFERS, UP TO 1933

(Source: D. H. Smith)

	Total	*New*	*Transfers from other parts of London*	*Transfers from outside*
Lea Valley	*100*	*40*	*56*	*4*
West Middlesex:	*204*	*91*	*100*	*13*
Hendon–Edgware	59	22	32	5
Park Royal–Willesden	82	37	40	5
Hayes–Southall	25	9	13	3
Chiswick–Staines	38	23	15	—[9]

At the 1951 Census the West Middlesex zone was still dominated by the same industries. In Table 17 the 1951 figures are compared with Smith's 1933 figures. The definitions of areas and industries differ slightly but broadly the figures are comparable.

Within the zone in 1951 there were concentrations of certain industries in certain areas. Southall and Hayes, as already seen, had the most unbalanced industrial structure, depending heavily upon electrical engineering, vehicles and food processing. These were still highly-specialized areas dominated by large factories. Nearer the centre, vehicle manufacture accounted for 20 per cent

TABLE 17
WEST MIDDLESEX: LEADING MANUFACTURING
INDUSTRIES, 1933 AND 1951
(Source: D. H. Smith; Census, 1951)

	1933 Smith		1951 Census	
		per cent		per cent
General engineering	5400	7·2	29603	11·2
Electrical engineering	12770	17·0	53421	20·3
Vehicles	19700	26·3	42049	15·9
Food processing	12280	16·4	30136	11·4
All manufacturing	75000	100·0	263789	100·0[9]

of manufacturing workers in Acton and 23 per cent in Brentford;
electrical engineering for 29 per cent in Wembley. General engineering tended to be more widely distributed than the other major
industries, perhaps because it was less concentrated in large plants.

The West Middlesex industrial zone: factors in location

In his study of the industries of West Middlesex in 1933 Smith
concluded:

> In common with the industries of the Lea Valley, the indus-
> tries of West Middlesex consist of the manufacture of products
> in which organisation and labour play a more important part
> than the value and bulk of the raw materials used.[10]

In West Middlesex, as in the Lea Valley, the primary factor of
location for most firms appears to have been contact with the market.
But in West Middlesex the market has two further aspects over and
beyond those already mentioned for the Lea Valley. First there are
the excellent transport facilities, especially by road, to the Midlands,
which supply many raw and semi-finished source materials and take
an appreciable proportion of the finished product. However, as
Bates stresses, it is wrong to assume that the road facilities were
directly responsible for the present pattern of industrial growth:

> . . . the ultimate pattern of industry was largely dictated by the existing pattern of communications at the time industrialization began.[11]

Thus even in Park Royal the large factories make full use of rail and even canal facilities for bulk carriage of materials and products. Excepting Brentford Dock (which has some export trade) Park Royal has the biggest rail-freight traffic in the west London area. The smaller firms are dependent on road transport, though in the central area of Park Royal, where so many of them are located, road facilities are very bad. Even where an industrial area is clearly dependent upon a main road, this is often a pre-1914 road, not an interwar arterial: the great concentration along Edgware Road from Cricklewood past Staples Corner to Colindale is the best example. The building of factories along the interwar arterials (Great West Road, Western Avenue) merely modified this basic pattern, but less than is often supposed.

The other marketing factor for the industries of this area was the close proximity to West End showrooms, because of the importance of luxury articles (as Smith called them) in the manufacturing structure of West Middlesex. The situation had not altered by 1952, when Bates concluded:

> The attraction of the London market is undoubtedly still the most important factor in the location of premises in West London.[12]

As in the Lea Valley, however, labour supplies were an important secondary factor. As Smith put it:

> The bulk of the factories are engaged in the manufacture of products in which the assembling of small parts by unskilled workers (mostly female), plays an important part.[13]

A pool of such labour did exist in west London, as in the Lea Valley. As early as the period of the Booth Survey there was a dense working-class population in the Notting Dale and Goldhawk Road districts, which then represented the farthest limits of built-up London. After the first world war the London County Council developed its large housing estates in the Wood Lane district. In addition independent working-class areas sprang up in various parts of West Middlesex, which is much less a homogeneous middle-class area than is commonly supposed. The 1951 Census social-class analysis showed that in certain areas, for instance Feltham, Hayes and Harlington, Southall, Staines, Sunbury, Willesden, and Yiewsley and West Drayton, semi-skilled and unskilled workers made up over 20 per cent of occupied and retired males.

The last important factor was the demand for space. In 1919 this was the only undeveloped sector of Greater London within a five-to-seven-mile radius of Charing Cross.[14] This was an historical accident of growth, without foundation in physical geography; for much of the land was gravel and brick-earth, which provided a good well-drained base for building. In addition the release for private use of former war-production factories, and later of the 1924–5 Exhibition buildings at Wembley, provided valuable ready-made factory space. The proportion of new firms was higher here than in the Lea Valley; but as already seen almost exactly half the firms Smith analysed in 1933 were transfers from other parts of Greater London. This proportion decreased a little in the late 30's, but still 61 out of 143 new factories (43 per cent) established in the West Middlesex industrial zone in 1935–8 inclusive were transfers from other parts of London. Seventy-six were new firms and only six transfers from outside Greater London altogether.

In the transfers from other parts of London, space was of course the important factor. Bates quotes cases. Glaxo Laboratories formerly had scattered works in inner London with a headquarters building in Somers Town. They moved to Greenford in 1935 in order to bring all their departments under one roof for the first time, and thus to allow simpler working. They needed to remain in Greater London for the sake of home and overseas buyers. Similarly A.E.C. moved from Walthamstow to Southall in 1927 to obtain more room. They could not afford to move out of the Greater London area because most of their products went either on to London's streets or through London's docks; and they needed to keep key staff assembled not too far from the former plant. The new plant on a 68-acre site was built wholly on one floor in order to reduce to a minimum the time and labour spent in handling. There were 2240 feet of private railway sidings for receipt of semi-finished

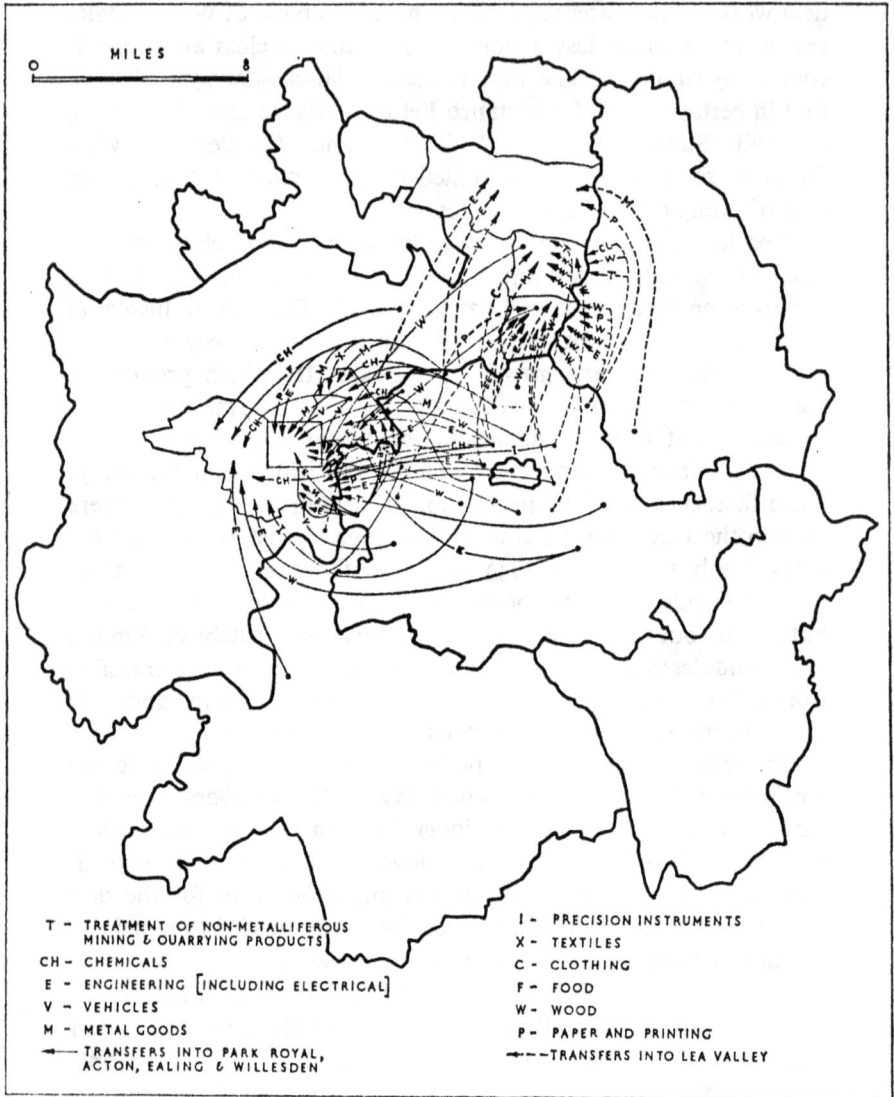

MILES
0   8

Fig. 22. Transfers into the Lea Valley and Park Royal–Acton–Ealing–Willesden from the rest of Greater London, 1935–8 (Source: Board of Trade, *Surveys of Industrial Development*)

materials—steel, bronze and aluminium castings—by rail. The effective market for most of the finished chasses was the London General Omnibus Company's body-fitting works at Chiswick.[15]

For the late 30's the precise Board of Trade returns permit detailed mapping of the transfers which occurred within London. In Figure 22 firms arriving from other parts of London in Park Royal in 1935–8, inclusive, are compared with arrivals in the Lea Valley zone. It is immediately apparent that the two sets of movements are largely independent and apparently unrelated. East End firms went in general to the Lea Valley, West End firms to Park Royal. Only in the north London districts of St Pancras and Islington does a margin of indeterminacy appear, some firms migrating westwards, others north-eastwards. Indeed the same patterns of movement are apparent on a wider scale. Of the 61 firms mentioned above as having migrated from other parts of London into the whole of the West Middlesex industrial zone in 1935–8, only eight came from the inner East End (including Finsbury). It appears therefore that the fundamental nineteenth-century division between a West End craft industry and an East End wholesale industry survived and even extended its ramifications in the twentieth century.

The precise reasons quoted by industrialists in 1933 as their primary ones for location in West Middlesex are set out in Table 18. It is revealing to compare these reasons with those given by the Lea Valley industrialists. In West Middlesex, transport facilities, cheaper labour and space were less important than in the Lea Valley, but the London market and existing buildings were considerably more important. To some extent the same differences would have emerged from a comparison between the West End luxury trades and the East End wholesale trades in 1861. There, also, nearness to the final market counted for more in the west; cheap labour and transport facilities in the east.

From these studies it does not therefore appear that the interwar industrial growth of Middlesex saw any radical departure from the principles which have traditionally governed the structure and location of London industry. Large isolated factories appeared here and there in certain trades, as in food processing and some branches of electrical engineering. This has however always been the rule. Because of their very size the works accounted for a great part of

TABLE 18
WEST MIDDLESEX: PRIMARY FACTORS IN LOCATION, UP TO 1933
(Source: D. H. Smith)

		Numbers	Percentage of total
1	Space: more needed for extension	30 ⎫ 63	10 ⎫ 21
	Cheaper land, rent, rates	33 ⎭	11 ⎭
2	Existing buildings	53	18
3	London market	68	23
4	Transport facilities	35	12
5	Cheap labour	5	2
6	Owner lived near factory	2	1
7	Other reasons, or unknown	72	24
		298	100[16]

total employment. But the adaptable small workshop continued to dominate the industrial scene. Forty-four per cent of the workers of Bates' west London area in 1952 were in firms with 500 workers or over; yet 38 per cent of total firms had four workers or less. The average firm had almost exactly 100 workers. The proportion of workers in giant factories (with 500 workers and more) was much less in older-established, more mature, industrial districts like Willesden, Ealing and Acton than in the newer areas like Hayes and Southall. The important factors of location for West Middlesex industry were the London market and the labour pool, as they always have been for London industry.

It will be most useful now to turn to detailed study of some of the industries which developed fastest in these outer areas of London during the twentieth century. Three are especially representative: engineering, electrical engineering and vehicle manufacture.

1 D. H. Smith, *The Industries of Greater London* (1933), 173.
2 Statistics on Lea Valley from Smith, ibid., section III.
3 Ibid., 65.
4 B. A. Bates, *Some Aspects of the Recent Industrial Development of West London*. University of London, approved for degree of M.Sc., 1954; unpublished.

5   D. H. Smith, op. cit., 77.
6   B. A. Bates, op. cit., 21, 23.
7   Ibid., chapter 8.
8   D. H. Smith, 87.
9   Figures from D. H. Smith, ibid, section V.
10 Ibid., 104.
11 B. A. Bates, op. cit., 3-4.
12 Ibid., 191.
13 D. H. Smith, op. cit., 104.
14 Ibid., 84-5. The fact was observed upon in *Report London Traffic Branch of the Board of Trade, 1910*, 19, which laid down the plan for arterial road development carried out in London between the wars, *P.P.* 1911, XXXIV.
15 B. A. Bates, op. cit., 192-3; *A.D.C. Gazette*, 3 (1928-9), 15; A.E.C., *'Regent' Omnibus Chassis at Charing Cross* (1930), 13-15.
16 D. H. Smith, op. cit., 85.

9

THE NEWER INDUSTRIES:
GENERAL ENGINEERING

Facts of location

THE first representative of the newer industries is the Census group
'Engineering, not marine or electrical'. It is a less extreme example
than the other two which will be considered, because it was already
quite an important industry, both in the country and in London,
in the mid-nineteenth century. Nevertheless the rate of growth has
been very high. Table 19 makes this clear.

TABLE 19

ENGINEERING: ENGLAND AND WALES, GREATER LONDON,
1861, 1921, 1951

(Source: Censuses, 1861, 1921, 1951)

	1861	*1921*	*1951*
England and Wales			
1 Numbers employed in engineering, thousands	106·2	597·7	826·3
2 Percentage of engineering to all workers	1·1	3·5	4·1
Greater London			
3 Numbers employed in engineering, thousands	18·6	95·5	161·1
4 Percentage of engineering to all workers	1·3	3·0	3·8
5 Percentage of London engineering to England and Wales engineering workers	17·5	16·0	19·5
6 Location Quotient for engineering in Greater London	1·1	0·9	0·9

140

Over the period 1861–1951, therefore, the rate of increase of the labour force was no less than 2·3 per cent per annum in the whole country and 2·4 per cent per annum in London. It seems unlikely that these figures are exaggerated by deficiencies in the comparison; rather the reverse, because the 1861 figures include large numbers of boiler-makers, many of whom should doubtless be included in marine engineering under the 1951 classification.

Within London, Table 20 shows that there has been a moderate degree of concentration. The local Coefficient of Concentration was 0·35 in 1861, and 0·31 in 1951. This seems to arise from two contradictory tendencies in location. On the one hand, there are large areas of Greater London which have hardly any perceptible concentration of workers. On the other hand, a few areas contain very powerful concentrations, marked by extremely high Local Location Quotients. In 1861 these latter areas were all along or near the riverside: Poplar, Southwark, Lambeth (probably partly residential; they worked in Southwark) and especially the south-eastern districts (Deptford, Greenwich, Lewisham, Woolwich). The Victorian manufacturing belt had only 39 per cent of the total engineering workers (cf. 56 per cent of all manufacturing workers). There was even in 1861 one marked concentration in the Outer Ring: in the Edmonton district, the home of the small-arms works at Enfield. It is notable that even at this early date over 10 per cent of the total workers were outside the area of the present County of London, a very high proportion for the period. The large concentrations seem to represent armament manufacture. Probably at least 15 per cent of the total workers in Greater London should be accounted as working in the Woolwich Arsenal, and another 5 per cent at Enfield. By 1951 the percentage of total workers inside the County had fallen to 50 per cent, which was much lower than the figure for industries like printing and clothing, but very much higher than that for some other new industries (cf. electrical engineering 33 per cent, vehicles 25 per cent). A quarter of the County workers were concentrated in the south-eastern corner, and this area of concentration had lapped outside the County boundaries into Crayford and Erith. But there were still appreciable numbers of workers in the centre of London. Westminster, Holborn and Finsbury together accounted for 10 per cent of all the engineering workers of Greater London. Outside the County, important concentrations had now

TABLE 20

ENGINEERING: LOCALIZATION WITHIN LONDON, 1861 AND 1951

(Source: Censuses, 1861 and 1951)

	1861			1951		
	Numbers employed	Percentage of Greater London total	Local Location Quotient	Numbers employed	Percentage of Greater London total	Local Location Quotient
England and Wales	106193	100·0		826278	100·0	
Greater London	18621	100·0		161066	100·0	
County of London	16611	89·2		80757	50·1	0·5
Westminster M.B.	971	5·2	0·6	8861	5·5	1·1
Holborn M.B.	347	1·9	0·5	4021	2·5	1·1
Finsbury M.B.	736	4·0	1·0	3288	2·0	0·4
Stepney M.B.	2086	11·2	1·4	1408	0·9	1·1
Poplar M.B.	1628	8·7	4·1	2251	1·4	2·2
Southwark M.B.	1704	9·2	1·7	5281	3·3	0·4
Bermondsey M.B.	669	3·6	1·2	767	0·5	0·7
Lambeth M.B.	1629	8·8	1·9	2723	1·7	2·9
Deptford M.B.	⎱ 3093	16·6	2·9	⎱ 2956	1·8	1·7
Greenwich M.B.	⎰			2712	1·7	1·5
Lewisham M.B.				⎰ 1043	0·7	0·6
Woolwich M.B.				13586	8·4	4·9
Crayford	⎱ 41*	0·2	0·6	⎱ 3991	2·5	12·4
Erith	⎰			⎰ 2270	1·4	3·9

					1951	
Edmonton ⎫				2468 ⎫	1·5	1·8
Enfield ⎬	1018	5·5	3·2	4205 ⎬	2·6	2·3
Tottenham ⎭				4185 ⎭	2·6	2·0
West Ham	597*	3·2	2·0	2011	1·3	0·6
Hammersmith M.B. ⎫				3126 ⎫	1·9	1·2
Acton ⎬				4190 ⎬	2·6	1·7
Brentford and Chiswick ⎭				2063	1·3	1·3
Heston and Isleworth	100*	0·5	0·2	2620	1·6	1·8
Wembley ⎫				6464	4·0	3·2
Willesden ⎬				5231	3·3	1·6
Croydon ⎭				6270 ⎫	3·9	1·9
Merton and Morden ⎬	64*	0·3	0·3	1270 ⎬	0·8	1·4
Mitcham ⎭				2882 ⎭	1·8	3·4

	1861	1951
Greater London Coefficient of Local Concentration:	0·35	0·31

M.B.—Metropolitan Borough

*—*Not* exact equivalents of 1951 areas

appeared in three zones, besides the riverside: in the Lea Valley; in West Middlesex; and in the Croydon area. The enlarged Victorian manufacturing zone contained in 1951 36 per cent of the engineering workers (cf. 48 per cent of all manufacturing workers); the West Middlesex zone had 18 per cent (cf. 17 per cent); the Croydon zone 8 per cent (6 per cent) and the riverside zone 14 per cent (5 per cent). The engineering trades of London have not therefore fled to the outer districts to the same extent as have other new industries, and to a certain extent they were never in any case rooted strongly in central London; while certain features of the location pattern, notably the riverside concentrations, have persisted remarkably over the 90-year period.

Factors in growth and location

The rapid growth of the engineering trades between 1851 and the present day is a simple function of technological progress. Engineering, like the other new industries, is largely a result of the second Industrial Revolution of the late nineteenth and early twentieth centuries, which depended not upon the chance inventions of obscure mechanics but upon methodical scientific research and its technological application. In 1850 modern production engineering was on the verge of a great advance. On the one hand, the principle of the prime mover was fully understood and applied, through the medium of the steam engine. But even this branch of engineering was to expand remarkably as a result of new forms of prime mover —the electric motor, the internal-combustion engine—in the later nineteenth century. What was still really in its infancy in 1850 was the whole concept of modern production engineering. On the one hand, it was true that:

> In 1775 the machine-tools at the disposal of industry had scarcely advanced beyond those available in the Middle Ages: by 1850 the majority of modern machine-tools had been invented.[1]

But it was equally true that:

> ... production engineering as we know it today was scarcely born in 1850 ...[2]

The machines had been developed, but they had not been widely and fully applied. So in London in 1850 axle shafts were still being made as they might have been in the Middle Ages, by means of a powerful lathe turned by hand; the process took several hours. A much more complex axle for a modern motor-car would be completed today in about 30 minutes.[3] The range of specialized machine tools for the performance of particular tasks has been greatly increased, aided by the development of new harder materials for the critical cutting jobs, while presswork has replaced machining in a wide range of processes.

The trade in London has suffered varying fortunes. As with many other trades, the forces that have governed the location of the industry in London, vis-à-vis the provinces, have governed also its location within Greater London. In the mid-nineteenth century London was apparently an important engineering centre, as a Location Quotient of 1·1 testifies. But it was engineering very different in character from what we understand by the term today; it was the slow and methodical work of the craftsman. Typical of this type of industry was the London fitter and turner who cut the axle shafts described above. He was a very special sort of workman, and even in the 90's still 'occupies a very fair position in comparison with the bulk of our workpeople'.[4] He generally came to London at the age of about 22, having acquired his early training in the provinces, married a little later in his home town, and set up house in the outlying working-class suburbs.[5] He was still, in other words, a pre-industrial craftsman rather than a product of the modern industrial machine, which indeed overtook him. Among his ranks were some of the heroes of the early Industrial Revolution, men such as feature in the pages of Smiles' biographies—Maudslay, Clement and Fairbairn. But already by 1890 the development of modern machine tools, manufactured in the provinces, had brought hard times to the London fitter and turner, though he had usually been able to turn to electrical work or to the manufacture of automatic machinery, which were increasing industries in London at that time. By and large:

> For some years past the tendency throughout the engineering and metal trades has been for London to become more and more exclusively a repairing shop.[6]

The manufacturer of engineering products was deserting London because he needed cheap space, which London was ill-fitted to provide. Labour costs and transport costs, whether for materials or product, were also higher in the capital. These influences, and especially the critical need for space, were driving the London industry out into the suburbs as early as 1820. Maudslay started in Wells Street, off Oxford Street, in 1797, and invented the slide rest for lathe work there; he perfected it in a new works nearby in Margaret Street where he moved in 1800. But he was forced to move again for space in 1810 to a converted riding school in Lambeth Lower Marsh.[7] Clement worked under Maudslay and then set up his own business nearby in Newington Butts, in 1817.[8] Fairbairn came to London in 1811 and took a job with Rennie whose works were at the south end of Blackfriars Bridge. Later he was at Shadwell and Greenwich.[9] It is clear therefore that the concentration of the industry on the riverside and on the south bank of the river (which in 1820 was still relatively neglected because of the lack of bridges)[10] was of early date, and represented a search for space which later drove the industry out farther and farther into the suburbs.

Engineering seems to have deserted London for the provinces steadily from at least 1850 until 1914, according to the New Survey. But between 1918 and 1930 the process was reversed. On the one hand, the cost advantages of provincial towns were progressively lessened as land values and rates rose in them. On the other hand, London suburban sites became steadily more attractive with transport development, including arterial-road construction, electrification of railways, and the extension of cheap fares for workmen.[11] More and more, the machine invaded jobs which long had been thought the prerogative of the skilled craftsman. This process took place largely between the time of the Booth Survey and that of the New Survey. As a result there was a great demand for semi-skilled 'process workers', which London's great labour pool could readily supply. The London skilled craftsman however found open to him an ever-increasing range of pre-production jobs in fitting and inspecting the automatic machines.

The engineering trades of London had by 1930 reached the form they retain today. In general London was the home of the lighter branches of engineering: lifts, refrigeration equipment, brewery equipment, motor accessories, stoves, gas meters, scales and weighing machines. Many of these were traditional London trades, which found their markets greatly expanded and their production methods revolutionized in the first half of the present century. Others again were new creations. The heavy branches, which were already concentrated on the riverside in 1860, remained there. Here, especially on the south bank, constructional engineering was carried on, and goods like cranes, hydraulic apparatus, boilers and tanks were manufactured.

1 K. R. Gilbert in C. Singer etc. (ed.), *A History of Technology*, IV (Oxford 1958), 417.
2 D. F. Galloway in P. Dunsheath (ed.), *A Century of Technology, 1851–1951* (1951), 141.
3 Ibid., 143–4, quoting G. Dodd, *Days at the Factories* (1843), 447.
4 J. Argyle in C. Booth (ed.), *Life and Labour of the People in London* (1892–7), V, 298.
5 Ibid.
6 Ibid., 294.
7 S. Smiles, *Industrial Biography: Iron Workers and Tool Makers* (1863), 206–7, 220, 223.
8 Ibid., 244.
9 Ibid., 309–11.
10 G. A. Sekon, *Locomotion in Victorian London* (1938), 7–8, 11–12.
11 *New Survey of London Life and Labour* (1930–5), II, 124.

THE NEWER INDUSTRIES:
ELECTRICAL ENGINEERING

Facts of location

ELECTRICAL engineering provides the most radical case of a new manufacturing industry. The 1861 Census statistics contain no trace of any manufacture of electrical apparatus, apart from a few manufacturers of telegraph cables subsumed under a general heading. Yet by 1951 the industry employed over half a million workers in England and Wales. This is markedly a metropolitan industry, and seems to have been one from the beginning. Indeed it is an important illustration of the fact that the apparent migration of

TABLE 21

ELECTRICAL ENGINEERING: ENGLAND AND WALES, GREATER LONDON, 1921 AND 1951

(Source: Censuses, 1921 and 1951)

	1861	*1921*	*1951*
England and Wales			
1 Numbers employed in electrical engineering, thousands	NONE	137·1	538·6
2 Percentage of electrical engineering to all workers		0·8	2·7
Greater London			
3 Numbers employed in electrical engineering, thousands	NONE	51·3	183·0
4 Percentage of electrical engineering to all workers		1·6	4·3
5 Percentage of London electrical engineering to England and Wales electrical engineering workers		37·4	34·0
6 Location Quotient for electrical engineering in Greater London		2·0	1·6

industry to London between the wars did not arise from transfers of particular firms from north to south, but from faster rates of growth of certain industries which had *always* been strongly concentrated in the south.

Within London, Table 22 shows that the industry is quite strongly localized; the Coefficient of Local Concentration was 0·47 in 1951. But to an extreme degree the localization occurs in the Outer Ring. Less than 33 per cent of the workers of Greater London worked in the County of London area in 1951. These were distributed fairly widely, with some degree of concentration in the West End, St Pancras and Islington, and the south-western boroughs. On the edges of the County and in the Outer Ring there were however some extremely strong concentrations representing large factories. The first was on the southern riverside below Greenwich, already distinguished as an important centre of heavy general engineering. This zone was centred upon Woolwich, which had over 7 per cent of the total for Greater London in 1951. Second was the West Middlesex zone, where Acton, Hayes and Harlington, and Wembley each had more than 5 per cent. Third was the Lea Valley where Enfield had over 6 per cent. There were smaller concentrations in the Barnet area and in Essex. Altogether only 26 per cent of the total workers of Greater London were working in 1951 in the extended Victorian manufacturing belt, and one-third of these were in the Lea Valley. In contrast nearly 30 per cent were in the West Middlesex belt, over 8 per cent in the Surrey belt and 11 per cent in the southern riverside belt. In its location pattern, electrical engineering is an extreme example of the new type of industry.

Factors in location

The present pattern of location within London evolved in historical stages, which depended upon technological advances in the commercial exploitation of electricity. It is notable that once a branch of the industry had developed in one area as the result of factors operative at that time, it did not as a rule shift afterwards. The first branch of the industry to develop was cable manufacture for electric telegraphs. The telegraph had been used in British railways as early as 1837 and spanned the Atlantic by 1858.[1] Cable manufacture was by its nature a heavy trade, and the final market of much

TABLE 22

ELECTRICAL ENGINEERING:
LOCALIZATION WITHIN LONDON, 1951
(Source: Census, 1951)

	Numbers employed	Percentage of Greater London total	Local Location Quotient
England and Wales	538599		
Greater London	183019	100·0	
County of London	59907	32·7	
Westminster M.B.	5374	2·9	0·3
Holborn M.B.	4760	2·6	1·1
St Pancras M.B.	2421	1·3	0·5
Islington M.B.	5618	3·1	1·5
Greenwich M.B.	4274	2·3	2·1
Woolwich M.B.	13081	7·2	4·2
Chislehurst	4072	2·2	4·7
Battersea M.B.	2711	1·5	1·5
Wandsworth M.B.	3580	2·0	0·9
Croydon	3693	2·0	1·0
Merton and Morden	3467	1·9	3·3
Beddington and Wallington	4648	2·5	8·5
Acton	11958	6·5	4·2
Hayes and Harlington	12218	6·7	7·2
Wembley	9375	5·1	4·1
Willesden	6498	3·6	1·8
Ealing	5722	3·1	2·3
Enfield	12007	6·6	5·7
Tottenham	2683	1·5	1·2
East Barnet	5712	3·1	10·1
Ilford	7034	3·8	3·4
Walthamstow	3156	1·7	1·7
Dagenham	3181	1·7	1·5

1951

Greater London Coefficient of
Local Concentration: 0·47
M.B.—Metropolitan Borough

of the product was the ocean bed. Thus in London, as elsewhere, the industry came to be located by the side of navigable water, so that lengths of cable could be taken straight from the factory and coiled in the holds of ships.[2] In addition the materials were often imported, varied in nature, and heavy: copper, lead, iron, rubber, paper, cotton, oils, bitumen and other pitch substances.[3] The plant itself was heavy and needed space. On all these grounds the industry established itself on waterside sites in what were then the outer suburbs of London, where land was cheap. So the Booth Survey could say of electrical engineering in London in the 90's:

> Much of the work is carried on beyond the London boundary. The construction of cables for use by land or sea is confined almost entirely to a few large factories in Silvertown and Woolwich. The employees live on both sides of the Thames, some within, but the larger proportion beyond, the census boundary.[4]

Even this first branch of the electrical engineering industry, therefore, pioneered the movement outwards to space in the suburbs, a movement which was to typify the twentieth-century industrial development of London.

Once established in the Woolwich area, heavy cable manufacture has remained there. In 1930 the New Survey called Woolwich 'a centre of the cable trade'.[5] D. H. Smith found in 1933 that, out of the 19 members of the Cable Makers' Association, nine were in London and seven on the eastern riverside.[6] The same situation prevailed at the 1951 Census, when nearly 39 per cent of the workers in electric cables and wires in England and Wales were in Greater London, and of these almost half were in Greenwich and Woolwich.

At the time of the Booth Survey, cable manufacture was the only branch of electrical engineering to have developed commercially on any scale. Otherwise scarcely a dozen years had elapsed since the exploitation of electricity had passed from the research stage. But between that time and the New Survey of 1930 a great expansion took place in the lighter branches of the industry, as a result of technological advance. First, there was a rapid spread in use of electric light and traction in the last 20 years of the nineteenth century; secondly, in the early years of the present century there was the development of bulk distribution of cheap power to move machinery. These developments brought about the growth in London of such trades as the manufacture of lamps, flex and light cables; domestic electric goods, such as stoves, irons, kettles, and wireless sets and parts; ignition machinery; switch gear; and accumulators and

primary batteries. By the early 30's D. H. Smith could conclude
that:

> The heavier sections of the industry appear to be located in
> the Midlands and the north, and the lighter sections in the
> south. This fact would account for the existence of fewer, but
> larger, factories in the north, and smaller, but more numerous,
> factories in the south.[7]

The 1951 Census analysis shows the essential truth of this assumption. Greater London had then only 10 per cent of the workers in
electric machinery in England and Wales, and 29 per cent of the
battery makers. But it had 44 per cent of workers in telegraph and
telephone equipment, 49 per cent of those in wireless and 52 per
cent of those in wireless valves and electric lamps. Cable-making,
already analysed, provides the only exception to the rule.

In 1933 Smith calculated that London had about 68,000 workers
in electrical engineering, or 34 per cent of the workers in Great
Britain. Trade lists showed that they were distributed among 65
factories. In contrast, 43,000 workers in the Midlands were concentrated in 10 factories.[8] This was a rough calculation but it undoubtedly points to the conclusion that, in the new as in the old
industries, London industry tended to be on a smaller scale than
its provincial counterpart.

Smith was able from his detailed records to analyse the origin
of firms in the industry in London. He concluded that there was no
evidence of migration from the north or Midlands. Even the largest
firms—British Thomson-Houston and G.E.C.—had been in
London for over 25 years. Nor did Smith think that London had
got a progressively larger share of the industry in the 20's. It had
always had the lion's share; but in absolute terms that share had
grown enormously.[9] The Census statistics show that in this also he
was right; for London's share of the national total fell slightly
between 1921 and 1951.

The reason for the concentration of the industry in its period of
growth in London will be fairly apparent from what has already
been said in general about the location of factories in the newer
industrial areas. The electrical manufacturers needed to assemble a
wide variety of materials and to distribute their products efficiently,
often by road. They usually wished to be near the London shop-

window. And they found ample supplies of suitable labour. In their early years the London electrical trades had the great advantage of being able to draw upon a wide range of skills from traditional London industries, then in decline: the manufacture of meters took men from the diminishing Clerkenwell watch and clock industry; the makers of electrical wire looked to the wire-makers and the brass-finishers.[10] Later the pool of semi-skilled machine minders was readily available in the London suburbs. Observers have tended to speak of such labour, often female, as intermediate in character between old craftsman and new labourer; but this type of labour, as already seen, was as characteristic of the old London industry as of the new.

The location of the industry within Greater London was a simple reflection of its need for space. Electrical engineering has from the outset been dominated by the large plant. In 1951, in the United Kingdom, the average number of workers per plant ranged from 80·5 for electric-light accessories and fittings and 125·6 for batteries and accumulators to 416·1 for radio and telecommunications and 625·7 for electric wires and cables.[11] Such an industry must locate itself from the beginning in areas where large factory sites are to be had cheaply. Between 1918 and 1939 this meant the Outer Ring of Greater London. The rise in land values that has taken place since 1939 would however make it difficult today for any large new plant to find a suitable site at the right price within the conurbation. In consequence this type of industry tends to go beyond the Green Belt and up to 50 miles from central London.

1 See the account in *Committee on Industry and Trade: Survey of Metal Industries, being Part IV of a Survey of Industries* (H.M.S.O. 1928), 279–80.
2 D. H. Smith, *The Industries of Greater London* (1933), 139 n.
3 Committee Industry and Trade, op. cit., 304.
4 G. H. Duckworth in C. Booth (ed.), *Life and Labour of the People of London* (1892–7), VI, 42.
5 *New Survey of London Life and Labour* (1930–5), II, 129.
6 D. H. Smith, op. cit., 138–9.
7 Ibid., 137.
8 Ibid.
9 Ibid, 138.
10 G. H. Duckworth, op. cit., 42.
11 *Census of Production 1951*, vol. 4.

II

THE NEWER INDUSTRIES: VEHICLES

Facts of location

VEHICLE manufacture was already firmly established in London in the mid-nineteenth century and the industry expanded very rapidly after 1900. But, as Table 23 shows, the rate of expansion was faster in the country as a whole than in London, so that the Location Quotient for London fell, from above unity to below it. As radical a change occurred in the pattern of location within London. (See Table 24.) Already in 1861 nearly 15 per cent of the vehicle-makers of Greater London were enumerated outside the present-day County—a very high figure for that date. By 1951 this proportion had risen to just over 75 per cent—the highest proportion

TABLE 23

VEHICLES: ENGLAND AND WALES, GREATER LONDON, 1861, 1921, 1951

(Source: Censuses, 1861, 1921, 1951)

	1861	*1921*	*1951*
England and Wales			
1 Numbers employed in vehicles, thousands	50·2	359·2	931·3
2 Percentage of vehicle to all workers	0·5	2·1	4·7
Greater London			
3 Numbers employed in vehicles, thousands	9·5	59·3	143·8
4 Percentage of vehicle to all workers	0·6	1·8	3·4
5 Percentage of London vehicle to England and Wales vehicle workers	19·0	16·5	15·4
6 Location Quotient for vehicles in Greater London	1·2	0·9	0·7

for any major manufacturing industry of London. The most important single centre in 1861 was the West End, where Westminster, St Marylebone and St Pancras together contained precisely 30 per cent of all the workers of Greater London. Within this area there was an industrial quarter of some importance in Long Acre. An observer in 1843 said:

> We are not antiquarian enough to know whether Long Acre has, from the time of its formation, been a bazaar for coach-makers; but certain it is that at the present day coach-making operations form the most remarkable feature in that street.[1]

He found more than 50 out of a total of 140 houses in the street occupied by firms calling themselves coach-makers or makers of accessories such as lamps, harness and fringes.

The other important centre in 1861 was the south-eastern quadrant of the County of London, where heavy goods vans were made by old-established firms to meet a regular demand around the docks. The manufacture of light vans, according to the Booth Survey, was scattered over London; carriage repairing was done in scattered mews premises.[2]

By 1951 this pattern had completely altered. The West End centre had all but disappeared; in its place were a number of very large individual concentrations in the Outer Ring, outstanding among which were Dagenham, with 17 per cent of all the workers in Greater London, and the West Middlesex industrial zone, with 29 per cent.

Factors in location

This movement reflects the great change which had already come over the industry in 1930, when the New Survey recorded that 'The rapid development of power-driven transport has revolutionized London's vehicle building in the last forty years'.[3] Carriage-building was by then restricted to wheelwrights and a few private shops, while large mechanized units had already come into existence, mainly in the Outer Ring, for the manufacture of motor-cars, buses, tramcars and aeroplanes.[4]

TABLE 24

VEHICLES: LOCALIZATION WITHIN LONDON, 1861 AND 1951

(Source: Censuses, 1861 and 1951)

	1861			1951		
	Numbers employed	Percentage of Greater London total	Local Location Quotient	Numbers employed	Percentage of Greater London total	Local Location Quotient
England and Wales	50212			931347		
Greater London	9538	100·0		143834	100·0	
County of London	8129	85·2		35556	24·7	
Kensington M.B.	577	6·1	1·0	2553	1·6	0·8
Westminster M.B.	877	9·2	1·0	2797	1·9	0·2
St Marylebone M.B.	997	10·5	1·9	1550	1·1	0·3
St Pancras M.B.	983	10·3	1·7	1931	1·3	0·1
Holborn M.B.	512	5·4	1·6	464	0·3	0·1
Southwark M.B.	612	6·4	1·2	1527	1·1	0·7
Lambeth M.B.	596	6·3	1·3	1363	1·0	0·4
Deptford M.B.				484	0·3	0·5
Greenwich M.B.	562	5·9	1·0	1889	1·3	1·2
Lewisham M.B.				1242	0·9	0·8
Woolwich M.B.				2644	1·8	1·1

				1861	1951	
Acton	} 248*	} 2·6	} 1·2	} 9268	6·4	4·2
Brentford and Chiswick				5230	3·6	3·8
Hayes				} 3736	2·6	2·8
Southall				4645	3·2	6·0
Willesden	44*	0·5	0·8	} 6929	4·8	2·4
Hendon	177*	1·9	1·4	7535	5·2	4·0
Croydon				3296	2·3	1·1
Kingston	75*	0·8	0·7	4861	3·4	5·0
West Ham				} 3447	2·4	1·1
Dagenham	258*	2·7	1·7	24564	17·1	14·4

	1861	1951
Greater London Coefficient of Local Concentration:	0·18	0·43

M.B.—Metropolitan Borough
*Not exact equivalents of 1951 areas

But, in the midst of this revolution, the methods of organization and even many of the essential factors of location remained unchanged. The construction of a bespoke coach in Long Acre in 1840 was in essentials much like the construction of a mass-produced car or bus in a large factory in the Outer Ring in 1950. Coach-making, the observer of 1843 pointed out, was a complex job involving the co-operation of many different artisans: coach-body makers, carriage makers, coach smiths, coach platers, coach beaders, coach carvers, coach trimmers, coach-lace makers, coach-lamp makers, harness makers, coach wheelwrights, coach painters, herald painters, and so on.[5] It used also many different materials in varying quantities: timber, iron, plated metal, leather, paint, varnish and woven materials. Wood was used in the body, in the under-frame (the carriage) and the wheels. Iron was used in the springs, and generally through the vehicle, to bear strain. Plated metal was used for ornament and for small pieces of mechanism (handles, hinges). Leather was used for covering the body, suspending the body in the frame, attaching the horses, and in a small degree for internal trimmings, which were mainly made from woven materials.[6] The materials and the processes were combined in different ways and in varying degrees, for the extent of vertical integration of production varied from firm to firm. Some smaller works were pure assembly plants, while the larger firms made most of the parts within their own walls. Making and selling were invariably integrated. A typical large firm in Long Acre had showrooms on the ground and first floors, a coach-making loft on the second floor and painting and trimming lofts on the third floor; subsidiary trades, such as plating, were carried on in smaller outbuildings.[7] Even the largest firms seem to have relied on specialist contractors for their wheels; the crafts of the coach-maker and the wheelwright were quite separate and distinct.[8]

The critical factor in location was of course the immediate retail market. In this, coach-making was a typical West End bespoke trade, just like tailoring. Though there is little direct evidence, it seems probable that Long Acre became the centre of the industry because it was relatively a low-rent area close to the then fashionable areas of the West End. Low rents were important for a trade which, then as now, was space-consuming, though the curious vertical organization of the productive process indicates that they were not low enough for convenient working. On this the Booth Survey said in the 90's:

> The combination, not easy to dispense with, of work-shops and showrooms in one locality, and the great space needed for both, coupled with the need of keeping up so large a place of business either in or near the fashionable quarter of the town, make rent a very heavy item in this trade. . . .[9]

Once concentrated in this area, the manufacture of the highest grades of coach developed there its own highly-skilled and localized labour pool. In the 1840's coach-making was reported as very highly skilled, and wages of three to five guineas a week were earned.

> Coach-body makers, indeed, rank among the highest order of London artisans: the number of first-rate workmen in that branch is limited, and does not appear likely to increase in any great degree.[10]

In the 90's, the Booth Survey reported, machinery had infiltrated into some branches of the trade, mostly in suburban van-building; but most coach-making was of too individual a character to be anything but a skilled handicraft.[11]

This situation remained until the revolution brought about by the internal-combustion engine created an industry geared from the first to mass production. This must have caused a very rapid change indeed, between about 1900 and 1920, in the scale of the industry. In 1851 the average carriage-making firm in England and Wales had only 7·6 workers (including proprietors). At the 1951 Census of Production the corresponding figure for motor-vehicle and cycle manufacture in Great Britain was 202·0, and over 65 per cent of workers were in establishments with 1000 workers and over. In repair the average establishment was smaller, 34·2, but even this represented a substantial increase.[12]

It is this increase in scale that must explain the dramatic migration of the industry during these years into the suburbs. Save for Dagenham, the western suburbs were the most popular reception area. In 1933 D. H. Smith believed that a powerful factor in the concentration of vehicle manufacture in the West Middlesex industrial area was the nearness to the chief marketing and showroom facilities of the West End, which in turn were close by the old coach-building district.[13] It seems probable that during the period of rapid change to powered vehicles the old coach-builders of Long Acre and the van-builders of the suburbs provided the nucleus of the new industry. Subsidiary trades, such as upholstering, changed the direction of their output and thereby became an important factor of location for the vehicle industry in Middlesex. If this is so, then during these years there was a direct link between the old industry and the new.

 1 G. Dodd, *Days at the Factories* (1843), 435.
 2 E. Howard in C. Booth (ed.), *Life and Labour of the People in London* (1892–7), V, 234–5, 239.
 3 *New Survey of London Life and Labour* (1930–5), II, 235.
 4 Ibid.
 5 G. Dodd, op. cit., 432.
 6 Ibid., 435.
 7 Ibid., 436–7.
 8 Ibid., 441.
 9 E. Howard, op. cit., 236.
10 G. Dodd, op. cit., 441–2.
11 E. Howard, op. cit., 242.
12 *Census of Production 1951*, vol. 3. For a full account of the structure of the industry in the 1950's, see G. Maxcy and A. Silberston, *The Motor Industry* (1959), Chapters II and VI.
13 D. H. Smith, *The Industries of Greater London* (1933), 88.

12

THE NEWER INDUSTRIES: CONCLUSIONS

THIS chapter complements Chapter 7. It seeks to discover from contemporary evidence the general factors governing the rapid growth of the new industries in London between 1918 and 1939. It asks also how far these factors resemble the factors governing the location of the older trades of London before 1914.

For these purposes the main source is the great volume of evidence given between 1937 and 1939 to the Royal Commission on the Distribution of the Industrial Population under Sir Montague Barlow, and the report of the Commission in 1940. The Commission was appointed because of the widespread concern in the late 30's at the apparently disproportionate industrial growth of London and south-east England relative to the rest of the country, and in particular to the then depressed areas such as Tyneside, south Wales and south Lancashire. From the statistics available to them, which excluded many workers in service industries, the Commission confirmed that this appeared to have been the case. Between 1923 and and 1937 the number of insured persons in Great Britain had risen by 2,418,000 or 22·3 per cent; but of this net increase 1,032,000 or 42·7 per cent had occurred in London and the Home Counties, whose rate of increase was 42·6 per cent or nearly double the national average. In the Greater London conurbation alone the increase was 703,000 or 36·1 per cent.[1] This was associated with a steady and substantial migration of workers and their dependents from the depressed areas towards London and the south-east, though a great deal of the increase in employment in the London areas was recruited from previously unemployed groups (e.g. females) within the region.

There was, however, no evidence that there had been a physical migration southwards of industry, in terms of actual firms. In an appendix to the Commission's report J. H. Jones showed that the rapid rate of increase in London was mainly caused by the fact that

F 161

in 1923 it had a much higher-than-national proportion of industries which were to expand between then and 1937, and a very low proportion in those which were to contract (the depressed industries). The Board of Trade surveys showed for the late 30's that London industry was growing mainly by the enlargement of existing firms and by the establishment of completely new firms, many of which should undoubtedly be regarded as hivings-off from established firms in the vicinity. Transfers from other areas were not important. Of 777 factories established in Greater London in 1935–8, inclusive, 560 were completely new; 202 were transfers from other parts of Greater London; and only 15 were transfers from outside Greater London altogether.[2]

The growth of London industry between the wars, then, was a self-generating process, and it is important to keep this fact in mind in examining the factors which contemporary observers held to be responsible for the location of the new industry. Four main factors seem to have been thought critical.

The market

Nearness to market was one of the two factors which industrialists most frequently quoted to the Federation of British Industries when it was preparing a memorandum to be submitted to the Barlow Commission in the late 30's. It was also given first place in replies to a questionnaire issued by the magazine *Business*, in 1935. In the words of the Federation of British Industries to the Barlow Commission:

> . . . the majority of recent new undertakings appear to have been of a kind whose raw materials are not produced in any special area, and the transport costs of which do not play a very large part in final costs. While convenient transport facilities . . . are regarded as advantages, they tend to take second place to the necessity for location near to the principal market. This is not surprising, since recent industrial development has been largely in consumers' goods for home consumption.[3]

Here the great advantage was with Greater London and especially with its north-west sector, which was newest to the West Midlands conurbation. Calculation from 1931 Census data shows that within a 100-mile radius of Park Royal were found about 18·3 million people. For Dagenham the corresponding figure was 16·0 million people; for the Kingston By-pass, 16·5 million; for the Sidcup By-pass, 15·6 million.

However, it is implicit in the statement above that the importance of the market is not to be measured in cost terms. It was admittedly argued by some witnesses before the Commission that the pattern of costs of road transport was a reason for the location of so much new industry within the north-west sector of Greater London, where arterial roads gave easy outlets to the great provincial centres of population in the Midlands and north-west. Road transport was most economical over relatively short distances, and its competition in the interwar period virtually destroyed the nineteenth-century railway policy of taper rates which encouraged the long haul and helped areas far from the market.[4] But any such theory based on costs is invalidated by the fact that:

> In the majority of factory industries, and particularly in those of the 'expanding' type largely represented in new factories in London and Birmingham, and making for a national market, the cost of transport of the finished goods is between 1 per cent and 5 per cent of the total cost of production, while the cost of inwards transport is usually, though not always, less than that of outwards transport. . . . In the case of an industry making for the national market, it is improbable that the variation in transport costs as between alternative situations within 100 miles of the centre of England would amount to 10 per cent of the total transport costs, or say 0·1 to 0·5 [sic] of the total costs of production.[5]

This conclusion was reached by S. R. Dennison, after careful study of actual cases. Elsewhere Dennison concluded:

> It is impossible to reduce these matters to terms of costs; it is only possible to note that firms do attach importance to situation near to the market, and that there are cases of firms which are not situated at the market being handicapped in competing with those which are.[6]

The importance of the market, he concluded, lay rather in the need for contact and for quick supply, especially where hand-to-mouth purchase was the rule. The same point was put to the Barlow Commission by Sir Edgar Bonham-Carter on behalf of First Garden City Association:

> I think it is more, perhaps, a question of time than a question of cost. If a factory situated outside London has an office in London it is convenient that the director can get there in a very short time. To some sorts of business, but not all, it is convenient that they can send in supplies to shops in a very short time.[7]

Or in the words of the representative of the Railway Companies' Association:

> I think it is just the fact of proximity to London and the London market, and the fact that they have constant meetings in London, that it is a common meeting ground for all sorts of businesses. These highly manufactured commodities in particular depend very much on working in with other forms of manufacture; the people concerned have constantly to meet and discuss matters. . . . I think it is the general proximity, everything is getting to be more and more centred, industries are becoming more and more unified and centralised, and the more time one loses in getting to London the less one likes it.[8]

Nor was the market to be conceived of merely in terms of population, the Barlow Commission decided:

> The importance of London as a market is not fully measured by its population. It has those advantages that are associated with a capital city—probably in greater measure than any other capital city. For some new industries London is the first market in point of time; it provides a sort of initial goodwill and is the first which the industrialist seeks to capture. It contains a large body of wealthy potential consumers and attracts many others from the provinces; these constitute the first approach to the national market. Further, many industrialists wish to be near

the pooling centre of experience and initiative and the centre of discussion and communication. Finally, the raw material of some industries is imported into London from overseas. . . .[9]

In particular, there was the function of London as a wholesale market.

> London is the national and world market for many commodities. It is the dominant market for many other commodities. It is a fashion and trade centre to which buyers resort from all over the country and from abroad. It affords facilities which no other centre can afford. It would be impossible to develop effective markets outside a single national centre. They cannot be decentralized without in effect destroying the market.[10]

These various aspects of the London market were undoubtedly a powerful factor of location for many manufacturers in 1938. What is unjustified is the assumption, implicit in the comments of many observers, that the factor was in any way new. It had the same character and the same force for many thousands of small London manufacturers, both in East End and West End, in 1850. But perhaps because these men's workshops were so small, perhaps because they were often indistinguishable from the residences around them, they seem to have gone almost unnoticed by contemporary observers.

Labour

The second factor, and the other most frequently quoted by manufacturers to the Federation of British Industries, was labour supply. But, the F.B.I. commented:

> The importance attributed to the availability of labour supplies may have a different meaning in the period under consideration to what it possessed in earlier times. Suitable labour now tends to connote adaptable and relatively inexpensive, rather than highly skilled, labour, and consequently industries now enjoy a wider range of choice of location than was probably the case in the past, provided they are able to find an area where the quantity of labour is ample.[11]

This was the result of

> the increased use of automatic machinery and the standardiza-
> tion of products and processes. Instead of the trained skill of
> the craftsman there is the more limited skill of a worker trained
> in a particular process.[12]

Or, in the words of the chairman of Slough Estates Limited:

> Semi-skilled. Machine-minder is the appropriate term.[13]

Commonly this was female labour, as D. H. Smith found for the
industries of West Middlesex.[14]

All this is doubtless true of the newer industries. But, as with
the market, it is equally true of the older industries—at least of
those that were mechanized with the aid of the sewing machine, such
as East End clothing after 1850 and East End bootmaking after
1870, and increasingly towards the turn of the century true of
trades long thought the prerogative of the skilled craftsman, for
example, printing. Again, the particular advantage of London has
always existed, and for certain important trades has always had its
special attraction. The difference between pre-1914 industry and
post-1918 industry is merely that the range of industries attracted
to the market and to the labour pool has become much greater.

Factory buildings

The third important factor for the new industries was the presence
of convenient factory buildings for rent. Convenience of premises
was indeed the reason for location given to the Board of Trade by
over half the firms that opened new factories in Great Britain during
the years 1934-6, and among those locating in Greater London the
proportion was nearly three-fifths.[15] There is reason to suppose that
the form of the Board of Trade questionnaire encouraged industrialists to select this rather obvious general reason. But buildings
undoubtedly were important for many industrialists in the 20's and
30's because, in the conditions of intense competition in the consumer-goods trades, they were often in effect launching a new

product upon the market; the risks were often exceptionally high, and it was a natural insurance to buy rather than rent the factory if possible. The existence of factories for rent, indeed, encouraged a new class of small manufacturer, according to the Federation of British Industries:

> There is this point. In the old days factories could not be rented whereas now a man may say, 'I will have a shot at it. I will rent a factory here and see how it goes.'[16]

Such a factory was commonly available for rent near London in the early 1920's as an inheritance from the 1914–18 war. The factories at Park Royal and at The Hyde, Colindale, had been government works producing munitions or aircraft. The case of Slough is instructive. The town is just outside the Greater London region as it has been defined in this book. It was built in the last year of the war as a lorry-repair centre for the Western Front. Because of its purpose the War Office stipulated that it must be near London and thus within easy reach of the south coast; that, because of the danger of air raids, it must be west of London; but that there must be through rail transport to the coast which avoided London; and that it must have level ground and a gravel soil. In a hasty wartime survey the number of possible sites was limited, and Slough was chosen as the nearest to the requirements.[17] After the war the depot was sold to the Slough Trading Company for £7 million.[18] The company was interested primarily in the lorries and only afterwards had the idea of a trading estate.[19] Thus one of the most important concentrations of new industry in the vicinity of London was originally located on the basis of strategic reasons of no peacetime validity. But whatever the original reason for their building, once in existence the factories became in themselves powerful reasons for location.

The spokesman of the Federation of British Industries quoted above was undoubtedly right in thinking that the rented factory was very important to the interwar industrialist. But he showed little sense of industrial history when he thought this was a new advantage. The tailor in Whitechapel, the boot-finisher in Bethnal Green, had invariably rented his home workshop.[20] The fact that 'his living-room becomes his workshop', in Beatrice Webb's words,[21] was indeed as we have seen a powerful reason in the development of the small-master system in East End industry. Again, the factor was no new one in this century: its range of application was merely wider.

External economies

The fourth factor of location for the new industries arose in large measure from the third: it was that, because of their origin as large government units or as exhibition buildings, the individual small factories in the new industrial areas were commonly grouped together, and thus enjoyed the advantages of ancillary and cognate industries. The external economies thus secured were usually general to all firms, no matter what their product, rather than special to one trade.

> On a Trading Estate it is usual to find 'on the spot' the services of Wood-workers, Packing Case Makers, Carton and Box Manufacturers, Printers, Foundries, Press Metal Workers, Electrical and other Engineers and Pattern Makers.[22]

The Barlow Commission Report, however, went further and declared:

> There can be no doubt that the existence of cognate industries is a factor of the first importance. . . . It is largely this factor . . . that creates the further attraction described in the evidence of the Board of Trade as industrial atmosphere.[23]

Where therefore an industrial estate came to contain a number of firms producing similar goods, a new version of the traditional industrial quarter was born.

Such are the factors that seem chiefly to have attracted the new factories for the manufacture of light assembly goods to the Outer Ring of Greater London in the 20's and 30's. It is clear that these factors are in general no different from those which attracted a range of older assembly industries to the inner London boroughs, whether of West End or East End, before 1914. The change merely lies in the fact that technology has in this century thrown up a great range of new industries where these factors have special force.

Lastly a word of limitation is necessary. The factors of location described above have for the most part been based on the judgments of the manufacturing and commercial world in the evidence they gave to the Barlow Commission. They may very well have been wrong in their evaluation. As the planners argued before the Commission, the choice of an individual manufacturer was not as a rule the product of a rational assessment; and it has already been shown that London industry expanded between the wars *in situ*, so that for most manufacturers no real choice of location arose. But in order to explain the history of industrial development in an economy where there was a free choice of location, it is unnecessary to prove that a factor of location had any real force: sufficient to show merely that manufacturers thought it did. For a study of London industry this distinction is important. London's most permanent economic asset has been her good economic reputation. Whether or not the Whittington legend has a foundation in fact, there is no denying its strength as a myth. The conclusion of the Booth Survey on London industry might indeed be amended to read: *J'y suis, j'y augmente.*

The Barlow Commissioners were, however, concerned to discover not merely what had happened, but whether it was economically inevitable. Here they found themselves ill-served with facts. Detailed analyses of costs in different locations were not available. In the event the Commissioners undoubtedly relied heavily on the evidence of S. R. Dennison, which has already been quoted. On this basis they concluded that a great deal of industry was relatively footloose, and could have been persuaded to locate elsewhere by a combination of control and inducement. In this they were probably right. But a new Barlow Commission, sitting today, would find it no easier to discover the facts. There are now valuable studies of precise costs in alternative locations for the clothing and radio industries.[24] In the broadest terms the conclusion of these studies is that firms which have opened branch factories in Development Areas have not suffered substantial cost disadvantage compared with the branch they might have opened in London instead; and that if allowance is made for certain artificial assumptions in the analysis the advantage is slightly with the provincial plant. These studies are, of course, of limited general application, and they take no account of social costs. These are costs of location in London which are not borne directly by the individual firm but indirectly

by the community as a whole. They include such items as housing
and rate subsidies, higher costs of health services and costs of travel
to work. They tend to be higher in London than elsewhere.[25]
Planners are now turning increasingly to the calculation of social
costs.[26] The sum is one which will never be added up satisfactorily,
but it is important to try to find an approximation to the answer.

1 Based on *R. C. Distribution of the Industrial Population, Report*, 24,
   164, *P.P.* 1939–40, IV.
2 Board of Trade, *Surveys of Industrial Development*, 1935–8 (H.M.S.O.
   1936–9).
3 *R. C. Distribution Population, Minutes*, Ev. of Federation of British
   Industries, para. 32.
4 Ibid., Ev. of Ministry of Transport, para. 10 and Q. 1885–1978. Bates'
   study of growth patterns has however shown that roads did not
   influence industrial development in detail: see chapter 8.
5 Ibid., Ev. Garden Cities and Town Planning Association, para. 18.
6 S. R. Dennison, *The Location of Industry and the Depressed Areas*
   (1939), 72.
7 R. C. Distribution Population, Minutes, op. cit., Q. 5357.
8 Ibid., Q. 5555–6.
9 R. C. Distribution Population, Report, op. cit., 48.
10 R. C. Distribution Population, Minutes, op. cit., Ev. of L.P.T.B.,
   para. 5.
11 Ibid., Ev. F.B.I., para. 33.
12 S. R. Dennison, op. cit., 76–7.
13 R. C. Distribution Population, Minutes, op. cit., Q. 2844.
14 D. H. Smith, *The Industries of Greater London* (1933), 104.
15 R. C. Distribution Population, Minutes, op. cit., Ev. Board of Trade,
   annex III.
16 Ibid., Q. 4384.
17 *Joint Select Committee on the Government Works at Cippenham,
   Minutes*, Q. 436–45, 3691–5, 3702, *P.P.* 1919, V.
18 *Select Committee on National Expenditure, 1920*, xx. *P.P.* 1920, VII.
19 R. C. Distribution Population, Minutes, op. cit., Q. 2848–50.
20 See for instance *S. C. Sweating System, Minutes*, Q. 8650, 8999, *P.P.*
   1888, XX (for tailoring); and D. Schloss in C. Booth (ed.), *Life and
   Labour of the People in London* (1892–7), IV, 90–1, 100 n., for footwear.
21 Beatrice Potter in C. Booth, ibid., 60.
22 R. C. Distribution Population, Minutes, op. cit., Ev. Slough Estates,
   para. 6.
23 R. C. Distribution Population, Report, op. cit., 47–8.
24 D. C. Hague and P. K. Newman, *Costs in Alternative Locations: the
   Clothing Industry* (National Institute of Economic and Social Research,

Occasional Papers, 15, Cambridge 1952); D. C. Hague and J. H. Dunning, 'Costs in Alternative Locations: the Radio Industry', *Review of Economic Studies*, 22 (1954–5), 204–13.

25 D. L. Munby, 'The Cost of Industrial Dispersion from London', *Planning Outlook*, II, no. 3 (1951), 5–16.

26 E.g. P. A. Stone, 'Urban Development and Cost Prediction', *Town Planning Review*, 30 (1959–60), 207–29, 289–311.

13

PLANNING AND INDUSTRY IN LONDON

ALMOST all of this book has been about the patterns of industry
established by the decisions of individual industrialists in a funda-
mentally *laissez-faire* economy. Only after 1940 did the government
make any serious attempt to affect industrial location in London.
Today, however, this attempt is part of the declared policy of
successive governments. This chapter sketches briefly the evolution
of the new policy, and tries to estimate its success.

The origins of planning policy

The post-1945 policy of government interference in industrial
location sprang from the recommendations of the Royal Commission on the Distribution of the Industrial Population (the Barlow
Commission) in 1940.[1] The Commission's first task was to establish
the facts. As already shown in Chapter 12, they concluded that
during the interwar period industrial employment in London and
the Home Counties had been growing at about twice the national
rate. The process was likely to continue, and so the Commission
concluded:

> . . . in the absence of some restrictive regulation by the
> Government, we find no reason for supposing that the trend to
> the South-East will be permanently checked. . . .[2]

The Commission went on to decide that such 'restrictive regulation' was necessary because of social, economic and strategic disadvantages which the concentration of industry brought in its train.
The reasons for this conclusion are too complex to be discussed
here: some were questionable at the time; others are now less
relevant than they were in 1940; yet others (for instance, traffic congestion and long journeys to work) are still very much present. The

Commission recommended the creation of a central authority to take national action, to include decentralization or dispersal of industries from congested urban areas, and the encouragement of a reasonable balance of industrial development (so far as possible) throughout the various regions of Great Britain, with appropriate diversification of industry in each region. They singled out the continued drift of population to London and the Home Counties as 'a social, economic and strategical problem which demands immediate attention'.[3]

Following these recommendations, between 1943 and 1947 machinery was created to control the location of industry on both a national and a local (or regional) level. A completely new Ministry (Town and Country Planning), as recommended in the Barlow Commission's minority report, was established in 1943; in 1945 the Board of Trade was given the power (with certain defined exceptions) to regulate the establishment or extension of industrial premises throughout the country, again following the minority report; in 1947 the Town and Country Planning Act vested complete powers to regulate land use over the entire country in the hands of local planning authorities—nine in all within the Greater London conurbation. The Greater London advisory plan of 1944 proposed the planned decentralization of over a million people and 258,000 jobs out of the congested districts of inner London, mainly out of the conurbation altogether.[4]

The achievements and limitations of post-war policy on location of industry may conveniently be examined under the two heads: national and local (or regional).

National planning policy

The aim of national policy has been to achieve a balanced rate of industrial development as between one region and another, which has involved the limitation of industry in the London region as a whole and its dispersal within the region. The extent to which this has been achieved may be judged from the Ministry of Labour statistics for the Standard Regions of the country. Since 1948 these figures have given a complete coverage of employment. The figures in Table 25 refer to 1952 and 1958, which for technical reasons provide the best period for comparison.

TABLE 25
CHANGES IN EMPLOYMENT:
STANDARD REGIONS OF ENGLAND AND WALES, 1952–8
(Source: Ministry of Labour)

	Employment 000s		Growth 1952–8		Regions as per cent of England and Wales		
	1952	1958	000s	per cent	1952	Growth 1952–8	1958
London and South Eastern	5259	5468	209	4·0	28·1	21·4	27·8
Greater London	4402	4528	126	2·9	23·5	12·9	23·0
Remainder	857	940	83	9·7	4·6	8·5	4·8
Eastern	1088	1258	170	15·6	5·8	17·4	6·4
Southern	965	1080*	115	11·9	5·2	11·8	5·5
South Western	1071	1143*	72	6·7	5·7	7·4	5·8
Midland	2020	2137	117	5·8	10·8	12·0	10·9
North Midland	1405	1500	95	6·8	7·5	9·7	7·6
East and West Ridings	1795	1857	62	3·5	9·6	6·3	9·4
North Western	2942	2982	40	1·4	15·7	4·1	15·2
Northern	1237	1299	62	5·0	6·6	6·3	6·6
Wales	916	952	36	3·9	4·9	3·7	4·8
England and Wales	18698	19676	978	5·2	100·0	100·0	100·0

* Estimate based on 1957 figures, due to boundary change which makes 1958 figures incomparable.

Three conclusions emerge. First, the attraction for industry of the south-eastern corner of England remains undiminished. Between 1952 and 1958 the area south-east of a line from the Solent to the Wash attracted just over half the total net national increase of employment.[5] But, secondly, of this increase only a small part was within the Greater London conurbation: one-quarter or 13 per cent of the national increase. Thirdly, in this period employment in Greater London increased by only 2·9 per cent—a rate lower than that of any Standard Region except the North Western. Expressed as an annual rate, this increase was little more than half the increase between the 1921 and 1951 Censuses.

Detailed industrial analysis helps to explain the nature of these different rates of growth (Table 26). It emerges that both in the country and in Greater London the expansion of employment in 1952–8 depended to an unprecedented degree on four industrial groups. Two were manufactures (engineering, including electrical, and vehicles); two were services (distribution and professional services).

TABLE 26

CHANGES IN EMPLOYMENT IN MAIN INDUSTRY GROUPS: ENGLAND AND WALES, GREATER LONDON, 1952–8
(Source: Ministry of Labour)

	Thousands (plus unless indicated)	
	England and Wales	Greater London
Engineering	205·5	26·7
Vehicles	139·9	9·0
All other productive industry	73·4	17·4
Distribution	307·8	79·1
Professional services	257·1	75·9
All other services	−3·6	−81·3
Not classified	−1·7	−0·8
Net change	*978·5*	*126·1*

The net increase in London depended more heavily upon these four groups than the corresponding increase in the country. Together the increases in the four groups equalled 92 per cent of total net increase in England and Wales, 151 per cent in Greater London. The chief factor in Greater London's low rate of net increase was the great counteracting drop in 'Other Services'. Whereas between the wars London's employment structure contained a high proportion of growing industries, in the 50's it contained a higher-than-average proportion of declining service industries, notably administration and miscellaneous (personal) services; and the rate of decline of these industries was greater in London than in the whole country.

For manufacturing industry alone the rate of growth in London was precisely half the national rate (3·4 against 6·8 per cent in six years). Engineering, vehicles and chemicals expanded more slowly in London than in the country; clothing contracted faster.

These facts must serve to moderate the comments which are often heard about the failure of post-war industrial location policy. After 1945, national planning policy concentrated upon limiting *manufacturing* industry in London, and even here exceptions had to be made in respect of smaller factories (with less than 5000 square feet floor area) and limited extensions (up to 10 per cent of existing area). Nevertheless, it appears that Board of Trade policy has had a powerful restraining influence on the growth of manufacturing in Greater London, and this in turn has influenced the rate of general industrial expansion there. Of the total increase of 126,000 workers in the conurbation between 1952 and 1958, less than half (57,000) were manufacturing workers, and it should not be thought that much of this increase was subject to Board of Trade control. Indeed, A. G. Powell has calculated that of total additional employment in the conurbation during this period, less than 20 per cent arose from schemes needing Board of Trade permission, and that most of this could not reasonably have been moved elsewhere.[6]

Local planning policy

The stated aim of local policy is decentralization of industry from the congested central and inner areas of London. How far this policy is meeting with success may be judged from the Ministry of Labour statistics for individual National Insurance areas within Greater London, which have been aggregated into areas to produce Figure 23. Caution is needed in interpreting these figures. They are uncorrected raw totals which exclude established Civil Servants and include all employees of large organizations which exchange insurance books centrally, whether they work in the area concerned or not. Nevertheless, interesting broad trends emerge. The most important are:

1. *An increase of 136,000 workers in central London.* It is this increase that has most attracted the concern of planners during the 1950's. Unfortunately there is no doubt that the statistics exaggerate it, through exclusion of Civil Servants (whose numbers have fallen) and inclusion of bulk exchanges of books (whose numbers may have increased). For the whole of Greater London, the raw figures over-estimate the increase by 78,000; if it is assumed that this error is concentrated in the centre, the net increase there is reduced to

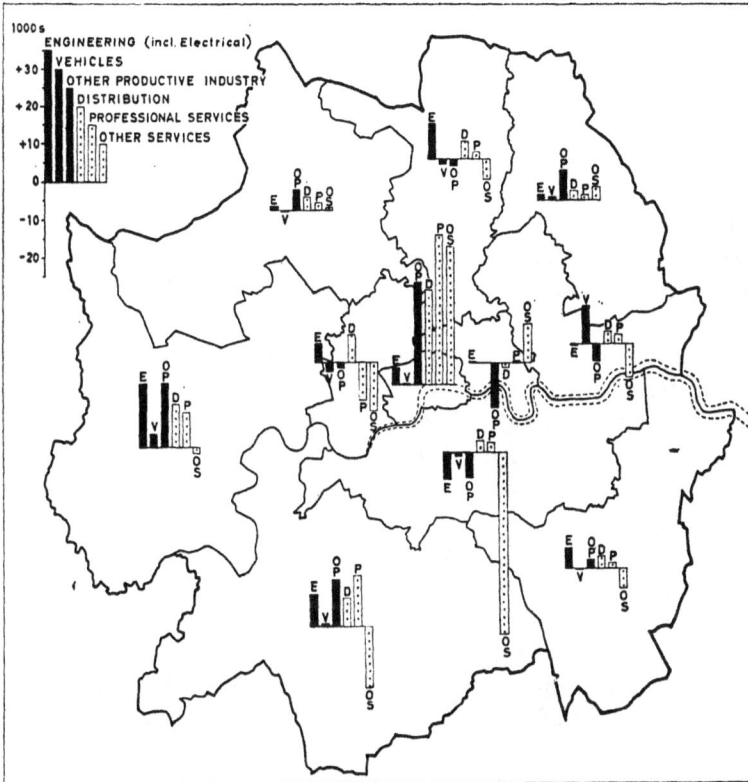

Fig. 23. Greater London: Changes in employment, 1952–8 (Source: Ministry of Labour)

(*Caution.* See important note on p. 176)

58,000. The raw figures show great increases in distribution and professions (a total of 66,000) and a total increase of 33,000 in productive industry; of the latter some 11,000 was in paper and printing, while most of the rest must represent either bulk exchanges or in-creases in headquarters-office staffs of national companies.

2. *A net decrease of 65,000 in the 'Inner Ring'* (roughly equal to the rest of the County of London). This figure is also suspect. Most of the decrease (48,000) is concentrated south of the river and at least half of this appears to represent change of practice in bulk

exchange of books. Nevertheless, it seems likely that there has been a limited contraction in this zone.

3. *An increase of 58,000 in the West Middlesex industrial zone.* Some of this increase may be due to boundary changes, but not much; 21,000 represent engineering and vehicles and another 17,000 increases in other productive industry—10,000 in food alone. There have been smaller increases in other parts of the Outer Ring, notably in north Essex (19,000, of which 9000 was in other productive industry—notably photographic materials and rubber), and in Surrey (27,000—mainly due to increases in other productive industry, distribution and professional services).

Each of these three types of change represents in some degree an important planning question, and must be discussed separately.

First, there is the great increase in productive industry in the Outer Ring, especially in Middlesex. This is a continuation of the interwar trend which was partly responsible for the appointment of the Barlow Commission. The rates of growth are difficult to compare, but it appears that in absolute terms employment in manufacturing in the Outer Ring as a whole expanded by about 16,000 a year between 1952 and 1958—the same annual average increase as between 1921 and 1951. In percentage terms the interwar rate was between two and three times as great. As Estall and Martin pointed out in their study of similar statistics,[7] most of this industry does not raise serious problems of nonconforming industry or journey to work. Under a fully comprehensive and rigid national planning policy part of the increase might have been directed to other regions of the country; but this Estall and Martin think doubtful. The verdict is one of non-proven.

Secondly, there is the decrease in the Inner Ring. The judgment here must be that the rate of loss is insufficient to fulfil the stated aim of decentralization within any reasonable period. Employment has declined at most by some 11,000 a year and more probably at half that rate. At the latter figure it would take 35 years to fulfil the aim in the 1951 L.C.C. Plan of moving work for 380,000 people out of inner London, quite apart from the compensating increase which has been taking place at the centre. In productive industry the loss has been about 4000 a year, and this has been highly selective. E. J. L. Griffith found that of 145 cases of decentralization within Greater London, up to the end of 1953, 50 were in

general and electrical engineering, and that this group had dominated longer-distance moves (29 out of 71 moves to New Towns).
The traditional 'quarter' industries, which often present the worst
problems of non-conforming industry—bad working conditions and
traffic congestion—have been extremely reluctant and short-distance
movers.[8] As J. E. Martin has suggested, these industries often thrive
on low-rent slum premises, and find it economically difficult to move
even to new flatted factories within the 'quarter'.[9]

The great difficulties experienced by the planning authority in
trying to carry out the decentralization policy have been described
by Griffith.[8] The most obvious candidates for decentralization are
firms forcibly displaced, either by bombing or post-war redevelopment. Unfortunately the rules of the War Damage Commission
allowed compensation only for rebuilding *in situ*—a major error
of policy—and redevelopment is necessarily limited by finance.
Otherwise firms may move for a variety of reasons, some due to
intervention by the planners: for instance, there may be a refusal
to expand *in situ*. Here the difficulty is that in most cases the L.C.C.
have not been able to prevent reoccupation of the vacated premises
by another firm, because under the relevant legislation no specific
planning permission is needed for changes of industrial use within
generously defined limits. Unless the reoccupying firm has been displaced by redevelopment, the complex of moves represents no re-
duction in total employment in the L.C.C. area. Unfortunately the
cost of compensation for control of vacated premises would be
enormous. In central London it has been estimated at £100,000 per
acre, and to move work for 380,000 (as foreseen in the 1951 Development Plan) would need 500–700 acres at £50–70 million. Griffith
concludes: 'the task of replanning the older areas of the County,
which can be said to have been started with the Barlow Report,
cannot be other than a long, uphill road'.

The third problem, and one that has attracted increasing attention, is that represented by the increase in employment in central
London. The L.C.C. have estimated that in 1951 almost exactly half
all employment in central London was office employment.[10] Apply-
ing this ratio, and assuming that the total net increase was between
58,000 and 136,000, this gives an increase of 29,000—68,000 in
office employment in central London in six years.

Until about 1955 this problem attracted little attention from planners. The County of London Plan in 1943 had ignored the problem; the Greater London Plan in 1944 dealt with it in terms of hope rather than policy; the machinery for national policy created in 1945–7 ignored it; and the 1951 L.C.C. Development Plan allowed generous increases in the areas zoned for offices. Even while the magnitude of the problem was being realized, no less than 44·4 million square feet of office space (new, replacement, extension and change of use) was approved in central London between 1948 and 1958. In the late 50's the average increase was 2·7 million square feet a year, compared with an estimated 1·5 million square feet needed for replacement purposes alone.[11]

The resulting controversy has unfortunately taken place in an almost complete factual vacuum. The subject of office location has been virtually ignored by economists, economic historians and economic geographers alike. The studies which exist[12] indicate that an office moving to a suburban or New Town location will save an appreciable amount on rent, purchase or building price for the office itself, but that this must be set off against higher costs of location outside central London: higher wages for key workers, possible lower efficiency of workers, higher costs of communications. Difficult of precise cost calculation as it is, the factor of rapid contact with the centre will doubtless remain critical for most central London firms. The dispersal already observable by 1961 is mainly into accessible sites within the conurbation. Development along the fast road link of Knightsbridge–Cromwell Road–Great West Road–London Airport is taking place at increasing speed, and will receive a further impetus from the construction of the metropolitan section of the south Wales motorway (M4). As Manthorpe pointed out in 1955, such voluntary dispersal points the way to rational government control of office development, through close study of trends in business enterprise, building development and land values—particularly the last, which government policy could help to redistribute within the conurbation to the benefit of employers and workers concerned. To try to divert much of the increase in office employment out of London altogether, however, would probably be foredoomed to failure.[13] [14]

The previous chapter concluded that for the study of the location of manufacturing industry there was a dearth of facts about precise costs in different locations. The discussion of office growth has concluded on the same note. In the 30's the Barlow Commission were troubled by this problem, and in their recommendations one of the functions laid down for the proposed central authority was research. Accordingly a research department was made an integral part of the Ministry of Town and Country Planning (now Housing and Local Government), and this department has produced work of the highest quality. In addition there are isolated academic studies of great value. But the findings so far are very limited, and the community is as yet ill-served with information about the precise forces which govern industrial location. In these circumstances our attempts at regulation must continue to resemble the attempt of an intelligent child to operate an atomic power-house. Much more research is needed, both on individual cases and social costs. In government and university departments alike, this demands more workers, more equipment, more money and more contacts between academic and Civil Service inquirers at every level. Only by the study of what has been, and what is, can we legitimately proceed together to the study of what might be.

1 *Report R. C. Distribution of the Industrial Population. P.P.* 1939–40, IV.
2 Ibid., 50.
3 Ibid., 202.
4 L. P. Abercrombie, *Greater London Plan 1944* (H.M.S.O. 1945), 33, 50.
5 cf. J. Sykes, 'Location of Industry and Population', *Journal of the Town Planning Institute*, 45 (1958–9), 126–33, based on the period 1949–57.
6 A. G. Powell, 'The Recent Development of Greater London', *The Advancement of Science*, 17 (1960–1), 76–86.
7 R. C. Estall and J. E. Martin, 'Industry in Greater London', *Town Planning Review*, 28 (1957–8), 261–77. This paper should be referred to for detailed analysis of changes in manufacturing industries.
8 E. J. L. Griffith, 'Moving Industry from London', *Town Planning Review*, 26 (1955–6), 51–63.
9 J. E. Martin, 'Industry in Inner London', *Town and Country Planning*, 25 (1957), 125–8.
10 Administrative County of London, *Development Plan, First Review 1960, Statistics* (County Planning Report, volume II), 40. (Definition of central area differs slightly from that used elsewhere in this chapter.)
11 Joan V. Aucott, 'Dispersal of Offices from London', *Town Planning Review*, 31 (1960–1), 39.

12   Ibid.; W. F. Manthorpe, 'The Limitation of employment in Central London with particular reference to employment in offices', *Journal of the Royal Institution of Chartered Surveyors*, 34 (1954–5), 389–99; 'Office Location in London Region' (Conference Report), *Town and Country Planning*, 26 (1958), 339–45.

13   See the argument in J. Westergaard, 'Journey to Work in the London region', *Town Planning Review*, 28 (1957–8), 59–60.

14   W. T. W. Morgan has made important studies of office 'quarters' within Central London. See 'The Two Office Districts of Central London', *Journal of the Town Planning Institute*, 47 (1961), 161–6; and 'Office Regions in the West End of London' *Town and Country, Planning*, 29 (1961), 257–9.

APPENDIX

EMPLOYMENT IN ENGLAND AND WALES AND GREATER LONDON, 1861, 1921 AND 1951 ACCORDING TO THE STANDARD INDUSTRIAL CLASSIFICATION

	Total employed, thousands					
	England and Wales			Greater London		
	1861	1921	1951	1861	1921	1951
I Agriculture, forestry, fishing	1905·9	1164·2	963·7	43·5	27·7	17·1
II Mining and quarrying	371·0	1231·7	741·5	0·6	1·3	2·7
III Treatment non-metalliferous mining products	105·9	214·0	291·8	8·5	17·6	33·1
IV Chemicals	19·1	214·3	397·3	5·8	56·2	95·7
30– Chemicals	11·2	116·9	268·1	2·0	28·1	55·6
34 Paint	2·7	18·6	36·7	2·2	7·5	14·0
35– Soap, Oils, Greases	5·3	78·8	92·4	1·6	20·7	26·0
V Metal manufacture	149·9	399·4	507·9	5·5	12·2	24·7
VI Engineering	159·3	1018·1	1564·8	31·2	160·1	357·5
50– Shipbuilding, marine engineering	53·1	283·4	199·9	12·6	13·2	13·4
52– General engineering	106·2	597·7	826·3	18·6	95·5	161·1
70– Electrical engineering	—	137·1	538·6	—	51·3	183·0
VII Vehicles	50·2	359·2	931·3	9·5	59·3	143·8
VIII Metal goods not elsewhere specified	274·7	346·1	445·1	29·6	38·8	73·8
IX Precision instruments, jewellery, etc.	51·3	95·6	142·9	20·9	45·4	70·0
X Textiles	1006·2	1153·8	868·0	28·4	23·3	26·8

Total employed, thousands

	England and Wales			Greater London		
	1861	1921	1951	1861	1921	1951
XI Leather, leather goods and fur	54·2	80·5	72·6	14·8	27·4	21·3
130-2– Leather, fur	30·6	46·4	47·1	8·4	15·3	11·4
131 Leather goods	23·6	34·0	25·5	6·4	12·1	9·9
XII Clothing	882·0	809·7	673·5	197·1	218·1	185·0
XIII Food, drink and tobacco	145·3	540·7	645·9	30·3	136·0	146·3
150– Food	106·7	377·6	485·5	21·4	95·8	108·5
163– Drink	33·7	116·8	119·2	5·9	26·5	27·9
169– Tobacco	4·8	46·4	41·2	3·0	13·7	9·8
XIV Manufactures of wood and cork	144·9	261·9	286·7	44·0	68·2	89·9
170 Timber	33·1	79·9	60·4	4·4	15·3	12·2
171-2– Furniture	66·4	102·2	161·7	25·8	38·2	63·4
173-9– Wood products	45·4	79·8	64·7	13·8	14·7	14·3
XV Paper and Printing	70·0	350·3	463·2	31·4	139·6	173·3
180 Paper	13·5	43·1	64·8	1·7	4·6	7·3
181– Paper products	6·9	64·8	90·7	3·2	26·2	30·8
186– Printing	49·6	242·4	307·8	26·5	108·8	135·2
XVI Other manufacturing	36·8	136·3	241·8	11·8	50·4	81·4
190 Rubber	1·0	46·3	94·6	0·7	10·1	19·6
191– Other manufacturing	35·8	90·0	147·2	11·1	40·3	61·8
XVII Building	497·5	753·1	1237·0	98·1	146·9	283·1
XVIII Gas, electricity and water	10·3	162·8	330·7	3·6	50·4	85·2

Total employed, thousands

		England and Wales			Greater London		
		1861	*1921*	*1951*	*1861*	*1921*	*1951*
XIX	Transport and communication	545·0	1392·9	1523·6	138·2	346·6	420·3
	220 Railway	87·8	548·7	463·1	11·4	111·6	101·4
	221– Road	137·4	296·5	458·0	40·3	90·3	113·3
	224– Water, dock	195·1	330·4	232·6	42·1	62·5	63·7
	227 Air	—	0·5	22·8	—	0·3	15·8
	228–38 Communications, other transport	102·2	204·0	334·8	37·7	77·5	122·9
	239 Storage	22·5	12·8	12·3	6·7	4·5	3·1
XX	Distributive trades	550·7	2022·4	2401·3	138·5	534·9	599·3
XXI	Insurance, banking and finance	99·4	239·4	402·5	33·9	109·9	186·9
XXII	Public administration and defence	193·1	886·4	1573·9	44·5	210·3	317·0
	260 National government including defence	156·5	457·6	1027·4	34·1	113·7	194·4
	265 Local government	36·6	428·8	546·5	10·4	96·6	122·6
XXIII	Professional services	273·7	788·3	1359·2	73·6	207·1	365·0
XXIV	Miscellaneous services	1550·2	2168·8	1856·7	372·6	483·4	484·7
999	Not stated, or ill-defined industry	346·3	388·2	17·0	63·0	45·0	4·5
I–II	PRIMARY INDUSTRY	2276·9	2395·9	1705·2	44·0	29·0	19·8
III–XVI	MANUFACTURING INDUSTRY	3149·9	5979·9	7532·8	468·8	1052·6	1522·5
XVII–XXIV	SERVICE INDUSTRY	3719·9	8414·1	10685·0	903·0	2089·5	2741·5
	TOTAL EMPLOYED	9493·0	17178·0	19940·0	1478·8	3216·1	4288·3

(Totals may not exactly agree, because of rounding)

FURTHER READING

There is no single work which deals with the whole of London industry within a reasonably compact compass; but there are (1) *single* works about *aspects* of London industry; (2) multi-volume works of *reference* which cover *all* London industry.

1. Single works

M. J. Wise, 'The Role of London in the Industrial Geography of Great Britain', *Geography*, 41 (1956), 219–32 (best introduction).

O. H. K. Spate, 'Geographical Aspects of the Industrial Evolution of London till 1850', *Geographical Journal*, 92 (1938), 422–32.

D. H. Smith, *The Industries of Greater London* (1933) (for interwar developments).

R. C. Estall and J. E. Martin, 'Industry in Greater London', *Town Planning Review*, 28 (1957–8), 261–77 (postwar changes).

J. E. Martin, 'Industry in Inner London', *Town and Country Planning*, 25 (1957), 125–8 (for industrial 'quarters').

D. L. Munby, *Industry and Planning in Stepney* (Oxford 1951).

2. Works of reference

C. Booth (ed.), *Life and Labour of the People in London.* Edition of 1892–7, 9 text volumes plus one of maps; Vols. IV–IX inclusive deal with industry. Edition of 1902–3, 17 text volumes including maps; the *Industry Series* has five volumes, four of which are reprints of Vols. V–VIII of the earlier edition; the last is an expansion of Vol. IX. Vol. IV of the *Poverty Series* is Vol. IV of the earlier edition. (This is an indispensable source.)

H. Llewellyn Smith (director), *New Survey of London Life and Labour* (1930–5), 9 volumes; Vols. II, V and VIII form the *Industry Series.*

INDEX

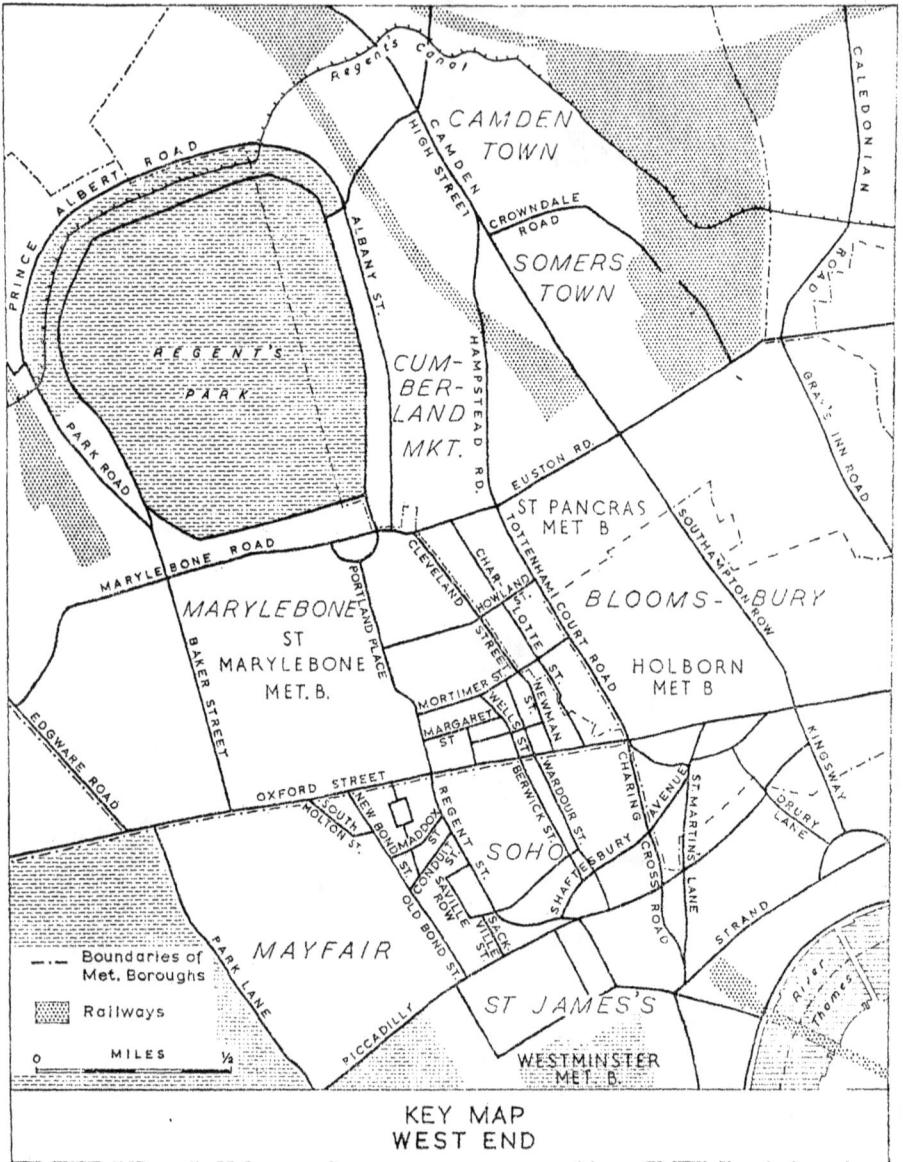

KEY MAP
WEST END

CAMDEN TOWN

SOMERS TOWN

CROWNDALE ROAD

CUM-BER-LAND MKT.

REGENT'S PARK

PRINCE ALBERT ROAD

ALBANY ST.

HIGH STREET

CAMDEN

Regent's Canal

CALEDONIAN ROAD

PARK ROAD

MARYLEBONE ROAD

HAMPSTEAD RD.

EUSTON RD.

St PANCRAS MET B

BLOOMS-BURY

SOUTHAMPTON ROW

GRAYS INN ROAD

MARYLEBONE
ST MARYLEBONE MET. B.

BAKER STREET

PORTLAND PLACE

CLEVELAND STREET

CHAR

HOWLAND ST.

CHARLOTTE ST.

TOTTENHAM COURT ROAD

HOLBORN MET B

EDGWARE ROAD

OXFORD STREET

MOLTON ST.

SOUTH

NEW BOND STREET

MADDOX ST.

REGENT ST.

MORTIMER ST.

MARGARET ST.

WELLS ST.

NEWMAN ST.

BERWICK ST.

WARDOUR ST.

SOHO

SHAFTESBURY

CHARING CROSS ROAD

AVENUE

ST MARTINS LANE

KINGSWAY

DRURY LANE

MAYFAIR

PARK LANE

CONDUIT ST.

SAVILLE ROW

OLD BOND ST.

SACK VILLE ST.

ST JAMES'S

STRAND

River Thames

PICCADILLY

WESTMINSTER MET. B.

- · - Boundaries of Met. Boroughs

Railways

0   MILES   ½

KINGSLAND

AMHURST ROAD

LOWER CLAPTON RD.

DALSTON LANE

BALLS POND ROAD

GRAHAM ROAD

HACKNEY

WELL ST.

DE BEAUVOIR TOWN

HACKNEY MET. B.

KINGSLAND ROAD

Railways
Boundaries of Met. Boroughs
Regent's Canal

0   MILES   ½

SHOREDITCH MET. B.

LONDON FIELDS

HOXTON ST.

HAGGERSTON

VICTORIA PARK

MARE ST.

HOXTON

BISHOP'S WAY

HACKNEY ROAD

CAMBRIDGE HEATH RD.

BETHNAL GREEN MET. B

ROMAN ROAD

HOXTON SQ.

BETHNAL GREEN ROAD

OLD ST.

GT. EASTERN ST.

VALLANCE ROAD

CURTAIN ST.

FINS-BURY

WORSHIP ST.

MILE END ROAD

MET. B.

SPITALFIELDS

MILE END

COMMERCIAL ST.

WHITECHAPEL ROAD

STEPNEY MET. B.

MOORGATE ST.

BISHOPSGATE

HOUNDSDITCH

GOULSTON ST.

MIDDLESEX

WHITECHAPEL HIGH ST.

NEW ROAD

WHITECHAPEL

LEMAN ST.

ALDGATE HIGH ST.

MINORIES

COMMERCIAL ROAD

CITY OF LONDON

CABLE STREET

THE HIGHWAY

R. Thames

KEY MAP
EAST END

For Product Safety Concerns and Information please contact our EU
representative GPSR@taylorandfrancis.com
Taylor & Francis Verlag GmbH, Kaufingerstraße 24, 80331 München, Germany

www.ingramcontent.com/pod-product-compliance
Lightning Source LLC
Chambersburg PA
CBHW061219220326
41599CB00025B/4686

9 781138 865112